RA

MW01516544

A Complete Guide For Beginners On How To Build And Grow Vegetables In A Raised Garden

TABLE OF CONTENTS

INTRODUCTION TO GARDEN AND GARDENING

Gardening is the practice of growing and also growing plants as part of cultivation. In yards, decorative plants are frequently produced for their flowers, foliage, or total appearance; useful plants, such as origin veggies, fallen leave veggies, fruits, and herbs, are grown for intake, for usage as dyes, or medicinal or aesthetic use. Horticulture is taken into consideration by many people to be a relaxing task.

Horticulture ranges in the range from fruit orchards to lengthy boulevard plantings with several different sorts of shrubs, trees, and herbaceous to residential back gardens, including grass and also foundation plantings, and even to container yards grown inside or outside. Horticulture may be extremely specialized, with only one kind of plant grown, or involve a range of plants in mixed growings. It entails active participation in the expansion of plants and also has a tendency to be labor-intensive, which separates it from farming or forestry.

Horticulture enhances life. It includes an appeal to our residences, brings a feeling of satisfaction as well as achievement, offers a healthy and balanced kind of recreation and leisure, or puts the unmatched quality of home-grown produce on our table. Horticulture may be natural and completed in restricted entertainment, or it can be treated as an all-consuming hobby. Regardless of the goals and also emphasis, fundamental understanding principles of plant society and also treatment boosts chances for success as well as brings enjoyment to the horticulture experience. This internet site is developed for the striving Idaho gardener as well as includes both fundamental and advanced gardening concepts. It offers web links based on locations with detailed garden information. It is a one-stop look for those that want to approach horticulture from an informed point of view.

He beeping of horns, tires fumes, as well as people rushing from one place to one more, these are the noises, sights, and smells that individuals who stay in city areas are revealed to daily. The one thing that individuals do not see in the middle of the hustle and bustle is an environment-friendly area where they can discover moments tranquility as well as relax.

There is nothing more amazing than putting your hands in the soil and experiencing nature, yet becoming one with nature is practically impossible for urban residents like Istanbulites. Blossoming, vibrant flowers, eco-friendly plants, and flower holders in various shapes are things that assist us in altering the ambiance in our houses, bringing us one action closer to the different colors of nature that we are until now gotten rid of from.

Gardening has been shown to have substantial health benefits and is an excellent means for city slicker to experience nature in their very own houses. For starters, it urges individuals to take part in inhabits and tasks that advertise health. When gardener decides to grow food organically, they are decreasing their exposure to pesticides as well as possibly eating create with higher nutrient content. Horticulture also lowers anxiety and also improves psychological health and also is considered a moderate-intensity workout, which can assist individuals to live longer lives.

House gardening has ended up being a progressively prominent pattern in recent times, especially in megacities. People that have no time or space for growing plants, or veggies and fruits, have started turning their residences right into tiny, makeshift environment-friendly houses where they can appreciate the miracle of nature. There are several ways to begin residence gardening, but first, you require to understand what you desire and whether you have the ideal space for the undertaking.

For people that are honored with a house featuring a small yard, taking up residence horticulture is as easy as can be. Flowers, veggies, and fruits can be grown even in a tiny garden, and you can appreciate bringing the food that you grow right to your table. However, not everybody can take pleasure in the thrills of a rewarding garden. So, how around turning among the edges of your home into a small greenhouse or a nursery!

At IKEA, you can find basic options for home gardening. The recently unveiled hydroponic kit permits you to grow plants, blossoms, and vegetables in the simplest way feasible. All you require is the best light, good soil, and also plant food for your plants. However, if you intend to grow your food in the standard way, there are a couple of things to keep in mind. Keep in mind that gardening is usually a process of trial and error, so unwind and enjoy with it.

Required for daylight Light is essential to home gardening. How much sunshine your garden area obtains will play a crucial function in your selection of plants for house gardening. If you try to grow a plant that needs a dark space in one of the most bright locations in your home, for instance, your home horticulture experience can go south in an issue of days. Therefore, be sure to do your study on plants according to the illumination in your garden area.

Make time for your garden.

The suggestion of taking up residence horticulture and producing an environment-friendly area in your home is fantastic; however, can you make the moment to look after them? Each plant has various requirements. If you are working too much or taking a trip a great deal, it is much better to discover plants that call for minimal treatment. Do not neglect that plants are living and taking breath animals. The animal needs to be taken care of, and you require to show them like. If you are not up to the mission or task, it is better to give up before also starting.

The pot impact Home horticulture is all about caring for a living creature and also creating a getaway to make your house feel homelier and comfortable. The pots that you choose for your home are as important as your plants. You can either pick ceramic pots or an additional type according to your preference, but likewise, take the requirements of your plants into factor to consider. The product that your containers are made of directly accompanies correctly how well plants will certainly grow, and also, some pots help plants to keep the water in the roots for a longer time. For that reason, remember that the ideal pot selection will undoubtedly aid your plants to live longer.

Spend time on your veranda. When we consider house gardening, the first thing that comes to mind is continually growing plants inside, but creating the first yard on your porch is always an option. When you determine what plants to grow in which pots, it is straightforward to transform your garden right into an escape area with just a couple of decor suggestions. If you have adequate space, you can make your yard a location where you invest your spare time at home with merely a table as well as some chairs. You can always choose hanging plants too if you do not have much space or are fretted about conserving area on a little balcony.

The devices you need Container yards, also called indoor gardens, are incredibly easy for newbies. For these, collect the appropriate pots, potting soil, a watering can, as well as a small trowel (or perhaps a sturdy kitchen spoon!) as these are the standard tools you will certainly need. For raised blossom beds or blossom beds in the ground, it is practical to have a trowel, watering can, shovel, hoe, and also excavating fork.

BLOSSOM GARDENING APPROACHES

There are two standard sorts of gardening approaches. Unfortunately, one of the most natural horticulture done today uses chemical fertilizers, herbicides, and pesticides. These chemicals made use of improperly can, over the long term, destroy useful dirt organisms and also toss flowers and various other plants out of their natural balance. This system of gardening focuses on dealing with plant diseases and even insects without reinforcing the plant's immune system and is damaging to the environment. Sadly, today it is practiced by many commercial gardeners and also farmers.

The various other technique is organic gardening, which functions to create an all-natural equilibrium in your blossom yard. This approach will make your garden as a living environment and utilizes the legislations of nature to create healthy and balanced plants that are resistant to diseases and bugs. Organic horticulture concentrates on building up the dirt, making use of plants intelligently, as well as maintaining a perfect balance. Natural garden enthusiasts acknowledge that microorganisms strike weak plants that reside in poor earth. An abundance of dirt microorganisms, from earthworms to fungi, give needed nutrients to plant roots and maintain your blossoms healthily and balanced.

Organic gardeners additionally understand that some plants grown together will benefit the entire garden-ecosystem. Roses and garlic are a traditional example as well as are reviewed thoroughly in guide Roses Love Garlic, by Louise Riotte. Likewise, some plants growed with each other might create problems for total yard health and wellness. This concept is called" buddy growing."

" In my garden, there is a big area of belief. My yard of blossoms is also my garden of thoughts as well as dreams. The ideas grow as easily as the blossoms, and also the desires are as lovely."-- Abram L. Urban

A home blossom garden is above all an area to develop and dream. It is likewise a location to play, to work hard, and to rest, contemplating what people, as well as nature, can create by working together. While it is simple to simply purchase blossoms like roses, daffodils, and also petunias, it is a lot more rewarding when you grow them yourself.

No matter the dimension of the yard plot you have to deal with, your time and also budget constraints, or your character, you can design a blossoming garden that enables you to meaningful your creativity, to obtain closer to nature, and also to even more take pleasure in being human.

Preparation and also setting up a flower garden may initially look like an overwhelming task, but discovering a couple of essentials will establish you on the path to pleasure as well as beauty.

HISTORY OF GARDENING

Woodland gardening is the globe's oldest kind of horticulture. Forest gardens originated in prehistoric era along jungle-clad river banks and the wet foothills of monsoon regions. In the steady process of families improving their immediate atmosphere, useful tree and also vine species were determined, safeguarded, and also promoted while unwanted types were eliminated. At some point, superior foreign brands were chosen as well as integrated into the gardens.

After the emergence of the very first civilizations, well-off people started to develop gardens for only aesthetic objectives. Egyptian burial place paintings of the 1500s BC are several of the earliest physical evidence of ornamental cultivation and also landscape layout; they show lotus fish ponds surrounded by balanced rows of acacias as well as hands. One more old gardening practice is of Persia: Darius the Great was said to have had a "paradise garden," as well as the Hanging Gardens of Babylon were renowned as a Marvel of the World.

Persian gardens were also arranged symmetrically, along a center line referred to as an axis.

Persian affects extended to post-Alexander's Greece: around 350 BC, there were yards at the Academy of Athens, and also Theophrastus, that wrote on pathology, was meant to have acquired a garden from Aristotle. Epicurus likewise had a garden where he walked as well as instructed and bequeathed it to Hermarchus of Mytilene. Alciphron also states private yards. The most significant ancient yards in the western globe were the Ptolemy's gardens at Alexandria, and the horticulture tradition gave Rome by Lucullus.

Wall paintings in Pompeii attest to specific growth later on. The most affluent Romans developed substantial villa yards with water features, topiary as well as cultivated roses, and also shaded arcades. Ancient proof endures at websites such as Hadrian's Suite. Byzantium and Moorish Spain maintained yard traditions active after the fourth-century ADVERTISEMENT and even the fall of Rome. By now, a separate horticulture custom had emerged in China, which was transmitted to Japan, where it developed into magnificent mini landscapes centered on ponds and separately into the extreme Zen yards of holy places.

In Europe, horticulture restored in Languedoc and the Île-de-France in the 13th century. The rediscovery of descriptions of antique Roman rental properties and gardens brought about the development of a brand-new type of garden, the Italian Renaissance garden in the late 15th and early 16th centuries. The Spanish Crown built the very first public parks in the 16th century in Europe and the Americas. The official Yard à la française, exhibited by the Gardens of Versailles, ended up being the dominant design of yard in Europe up until the middle of the 18th century when it was replaced by the English landscape garden and the French landscaped yard.

The 19th century saw an uproar of historic resurgences and Romantic cottage-inspired horticulture. In England, William Robinson, as well as Gertrude Jekyll, were reliable supporters of the wild garden and also the perennial garden specifically. Andrew Jackson Downing and also Frederick Regulation Olmsted adapted European styles for North America, mainly affecting public parks, campuses, and suburban landscapes. Olmsted's influence prolonged well right into the 20th century.

The 20th century saw the impact of modernism in the yard: from the articulate quality of Thomas Church on the vibrant shades and kinds of Brazilian Roberto Burle Marx. Keen ecological awareness and also Lasting layout methods, such as environment-friendly roof coverings and even rain harvesting, are driving brand-new factors to consider in gardening today.

Egyptian Gardens

Gardens were much valued in the Egyptian times and also were kept both for nonreligious objectives and connected to temple substances. Gardens' secretive residences, as well as rental properties before the New Kingdom, were primarily used for growing veggies and also situated near a canal or the river. Nonetheless, in the New Kingdom, they were commonly bordered by wall surfaces as well as their objective incorporated satisfaction as well as appeal besides utility. Yard create made out an integral part of food items, yet blossoms were also grown for use in garlands to use at festive occasions and also for medicinal objectives. While the bad maintained a spot for growing vegetables, the abundant people can pay for gardens lined with sheltering trees and even ornamental swimming pools with fish and waterfowl. There could be wooden structures developing pergolas to support creeping plants of grapes where raisins and a glass of wine were created. There might also be fancy rock kiosks for ornamental factors, with ornamental statuaries.

Temple gardens had stories for cultivating particular vegetables, plants or herbs taken into consideration sacred to a specific being of the divine as well as which were needed in routines and offerings like lettuce to Min. Spiritual groves and ornamental trees were planted in front of or near both cult temples as well as mortuary temples. As holy places were depictions of heaven and built as the real home of the god, yards were set out according to the very same principle. Methods leading up to the entrance could be lined with trees, yards might hold small yards as well as in between holy place buildings yards with trees, vineyards, flowers as well as ponds were kept.

The ancient Egyptian garden would undoubtedly have looked various to a modern-day viewer than a garden in our days. It would indeed have seemed a lot more like a collection of herbs or a spot of wildflowers, lacking the specially bred blossoms of today. Flowers, like the iris, chrysanthemum, lily, and delphinium (blue), were known to the ancients however do not include much in yard scenes. Official bouquets appear to have been made up of mandrake, poppy, cornflower, and also or lotus as well as papyrus.

Due to the arid environment of Egypt, tending gardens meant constant attention as well as depended on watering. Temples and houses of the wealthy used skilled gardeners. Responsibilities consisted of planting, weeding, sprinkling using a shaduf, pruning of fruit trees, excavating the ground, harvesting the fruit, etc

Persian Gardens All Persian yards, from the ancient to the high classic was developed in opposition to the severe as well as a dry landscape of the Iranian Plateau. Unlike historical European gardens, which seemed carved or re-ordered from within their existing landscape, Persian yards looked like unfeasibilities. Their ethereal and delicate top qualities stressed their innate comparison to the aggressive environment.

The heart of Persia, modern Iran, is high and dry. Mikayla is impressive A collection of containers, as well as plateaus, are separated by the two leading chains of mountains, the Alborz and also the Zagros. Considering that old times, lush yards have grown in the region because of an ingenious design system of below ground aqueducts called qanats. Originating in northeastern Iran around 800 BC, qanats brought the water from the snowmelt to the plains for watering and human usage.

The very existence, as well as the wealth of water, became the significance of the Persian yard. A wide variety of varieties thrived while slim networks supplied water throughout the yard, feeding water fountains and pools, cooling the ambiance, and providing tender, constant music airborne. Although gardens were areas for poetry, reflection, and privacy, they were not limited to the enjoyment and also a haven. Throughout Persia's background, gardens were central to the political life of the gentility. The Achaemenian king Cyrus positioned his throne within his yard at Pasargadae. Persian miniature paints from the 15th to the 17th century depict kings obtaining diplomats in their yards, treaties being signed there, banquets as well as celebrations, and all defining moments of national identity along with portrayals of legendary enjoys. The illustrated history, Shahnameh, Book of Kings, information both the dreamy and the useful in court life.

The ancient yards before Cyrus and those of his offspring show evidence of the features that remained to specify yards in Persia and also in a position that drew on Persian concepts, from India to Spain. Gardens commonly were divided into quadrants by networks of water, frequently punctuated by geometrically shaped basins. At the main intersection point was a platform for seeing, which later on developed into a formal open structure, often decorated with coffered ceiling structures that represented the complexity of the heavens. Geometry as a presentation of the gotten universe was commemorated throughout Persian yards from the surface style includes to the fundamental ground plane and also its fourfold Chahar bagh layout, standing for the four edges of the globe in the old vernacular, and even the four rivers of heaven a lot more predominately connected with the Islamic period. The roots of an earthly paradise, however, come from Mesopotamia hundreds of years before the Achaemenians, long before the Islamic duration. Persian layout aspects confirmed to have a natural fondness to certain Islamic principles; however, because they were so deeply embedded in the society of the area, they kept their Persian-ness throughout the nation's troubled history.

The connection of style to the Persian garden is layered, influenced by climate and also geography, and also infused with a feeling of the ephemeral top qualities of light and even representation. The boundary in between exterior and interior spaces was porous as well as often clear via making use of carved displays, deep archways, several vaults as well as honeycomb-patterned ceilings punctured with tiny windows of light. Via these tools, the rock, mud as well as ceramic products look like delicate as well as malleable as paper, conveying the top fugitive qualities of light and also shadow while playing with what is disclosed and also what is veiled.

Classic Persian yards were lived areas, one picture that they are best seen from within. As 17th-century European gardens expressed the idea of a fortunate point of view as demonstrated in a Renaissance painting, Persian yards can additionally be viewed about their classical tradition of art throughout the Safavid period, contemporaneous of the European Renaissance. Where the area of the paints appears flat and perplexing, an equilibrium is found in several entrance points and equal attention to every detail, whether it is the king's action, a servant's gesture, or the ruby red of a dish of pomegranates. Regardless of a hierarchical, feudal culture, whatever is repainted equally and also in sharp focus. As the audience, you go to when inside and almost everywhere.

The Islamic yards of Spain created throughout the 14th century are far more elaborate as well as extensive than north European gardens of that period. Including open yard areas, intricate floor tile designs, water functions, and also sculpture, the layouts were affected by the Moors. Unlike the medieval yards depicted above, these gardens were elegant exterior rooms where participants of the court might convene and also cool themselves from the intense heat of the sunlight. The Alhambra Palace, as well as the Generalife gardens that border the royal residence in Granada, Spain, make it through today as perfect examples of the mark of Arabic society on Spanish architecture and landscape layout.

Hellenistic Gardens

It wonders that although the Egyptians, as well as Romans both, gardened with vigor, the Greeks did not own personal yards. They did put yards around holy places, and they decorated walkways and also roads with sculptures. Yet, the elaborate and even pleasure gardens that showed wealth in the other neighborhoods are seemingly absent.

TYPES OF GARDENING

The residential yard can presume nearly any identification the owner desires within the limits of the environment, products, and implies. The dimension of the story is among the primary factors, deciding not only the scope yet also the kind of display screen as well as use. Limitations on a room near city centers, along with the dream to spend less time on maintenance, have often tended to make modern-day gardens ever before smaller. Paradoxically, this occurs when the selection of plants, as well as hybrids, has never been broader. The smart tiny garden enthusiast stays clear of the lures of this reception. Several of one of the most attractive miniature systems, such as those seen in Japan or some Western outdoor patio yards, is successfully based on an ascetic simplicity of design and material, with a handful of plants offered area to discover their true identities.

In the medium- to large-sized garden, the custom usually continues of dividing the area to serve different purposes: a primary ornamental area to enhance the residence and also give panoramas; walkways as well as seating locations for recreation; a vegetable plot; a kids' play area; and includes to stand out occasionally. Because most yards are blended, the resulting style refers to emphasis as opposed to unique concentration on one aspect. It may serve to assess the primary garden kinds briefly.

Flower gardens

Though blossom gardens in various nations might vary in the types of plants that are grown, the central planning as well as principles are nearly the very same, whether the yards are formal or casual. Trees and bushes are the pillars of an adequately designed flower garden. These long-term attributes are generally prepared first, and the areas for herbaceous plants, annuals, and also bulbs are set up around them. The variety of blooming trees and also bushes are enormous. It is essential, however, that such plants be appropriate to the locations they will undoubtedly occupy when mature. Therefore it is of little use to grow a woodland tree that will grow 100 feet (30 meters) high and also 50 feet across in a small suburban front garden 30 feet square, yet a slim flowering cherry or redbud tree would undoubtedly be quite suitable.

Blending as well as comparison of color along with forms are necessary aspects to take into consideration in intending a yard. The older kind of floral border was made to provide a maximum screen of color in summer. However, lots of gardeners now choose to have flowers throughout the very early spring as well, at the cost of some bare patches later on. This is usually done by planting early-flowering light bulbs in teams towards the front. Mixed borders of blooming hedges combined with herbaceous plants are likewise prominent and do not need rather so much maintenance as the herbaceous border.

Teams of half-hardy annuals, which can hold up against low night temperatures, might be planted at the end of springtime to load voids left by the spring-flowering bulbs. The perpetual-flowering roses and also a few of the bigger hedge roses look great toward the rear of such a boundary. Yet, the crossbreed tea roses, as well as the floribunda as well as polyantha roses, are typically growed in separate rose beds or a rose garden on their own.

Woodland gardens

The casual forest yard is the natural offspring of the shrubby "wild" of earlier times. The significance of the woodland garden is informality as well as naturalness—courses curve as opposed to run straight and also are of mulch or grass rather than pavement. Trees are thinned to permit adequate light, particularly in the meadows, yet uneven teams might be left, and any type of mature tree of personality can be a focal point. Plants are chosen dramatically from those that are woodlanders in their native countries: rhododendron, magnolia, Pieris, as well as maple amongst the trees and hedges; lily, daffodil, and snowdrop amongst the bulbs; primrose, hellebore, St.-John's- wort, epimedium, and several others among the natural herbs.

Rock yards

Rock yards are designed to appear. They are a natural part of a rough hill or slope. If rocks are included, they are typically laid on their more prominent edges, as in natural strata. A few large stones usually look far better than many small rocks. In a properly designed rock yard, foundations are organized so that there are various direct exposures for sun-tolerant plants such as rockroses as well as for shade-tolerant plants such as primulas, which frequently do better in an impressive, north-facing facet. Numerous smaller perennial plants are available for filling up spaces in upright fractures among the rock faces.

The primary rocks from which rock yards are created are sandstone and also limestone. Sandstone, less uneven as well as pitted typically, looks more relaxed as well as natural, however specific plants, significantly most of the dianthuses, do most beautiful in sedimentary rock. Granite is generally considered as too hard as well as unsuitable for the rock garden since it weathers exceptionally slowly.

Water yards

The water yard represents the earliest forms of horticulture—Egyptian records as well as pictures of grown water lilies day as far back as 2000 BCE. The Japanese have likewise made water gardens to their own specific and also stunning patterns for many centuries. Many have an ornamental light of stone in the center or possibly a flat trellis roof of wisteria crossing the water.

In Europe and The United States and Canada, water yards range from formal pools with a rectangular or round overview, often with fountains in the center as well as commonly without plants or with merely one or two water lilies (Nymphaea), to natural swimming pools of irregular summary grown with water lilies and also other water plants as well as surrounded by boggy or damp soil where moisture-tolerant plants can be growed. The pool has to include appropriate oxygenating plants to maintain the water clear as well as support any type of presented fish. Many water plants, consisting of even the giant water lilies, do well in still water two to five feet deep. Pleasant water lilies blossom throughout the day, yet many of the exotic, as well as subtropical zones, open their blossoms only in the evening.

In civilized nations, water gardens likewise can be made under glass, and also the swimming pools can be maintained heated. In such cases, even more, tropical plants, such as the fantastic Victoria amazonica or the lotus, can be grown with papyrus reeds at the side. The series of moisture-loving plants for damp locations beside the swimming pool is excellent and consists of numerous gorgeous plants such as the candlestick primulas, calas, irises, and osmunda ferns.

Herb and vegetable gardens

A lot of the gardens of the middle ages, as well as the very first botanical gardens, were exceedingly natural herb gardens having plants utilized for medical purposes or natural herbs such as thyme, parsley, rosemary, fennel, marjoram, as well as dill for savoring foods. The term natural herb yard is typically made use of currently to represent a garden of herbs used for food preparation, and also the medical facet is seldom considered. Herb gardens require a sunny position since most of the plants grown are native to warm, arid regions.

The vegetable garden also needs an open and sunny location. Great growing and prep work of the ground are essential for successful veggie expansion, and also, it is additionally preferable to practice a turning of plants as in farming. The typical period of turning for vegetables is three years; this likewise helps to prevent the carryover from period to period of specific pests and diseases.

The old French potager, the prized veggie garden, was

grown to be decorative as well as valuable; the short rows with little hedges around and the high requirement of cultivation stand for a version of the art of vegetable growing. The fancy parterre vegetable garden at the Château de Villandry is maybe the most beautiful example in Europe of a decorative vegetable yard.

Roof covering gardens

The modern-day tendency in style for level roof coverings has implemented the growth of eye-catching roof covering gardens in urban locations over private residences and also industrial buildings. These yards adhere to the same principles as others other than that the deepness of dirt is minimum, to keep the weight on the roof reduced, and as a result, the dimension of plants is restricted. The plants are usually set in bathtubs, or other containers, however, intricate roof covering yards have been made with little pools and beds. Beds of flowering plants are suitable for it, among which may be stood bathtubs of sampling plants to generate a wanted result.

Fragrant gardens

The aroma is one of the top qualities that lots of people value highly in yards. Fragrant yards, in which aroma from leaves or flowers is the primary criterion for the addition of a plant, have been established, mainly for the advantage of blind individuals. Some plants release a strong scent completely sunlight, and also lots of must be bruised or massaged to yield their fragrance. These are generally grown in elevated beds within easy reach of visitors.

TOOLS FOR GARDENING

Hand Trowel

Whether you're gardening in containers, increased beds, or straight in your backyard, a hand trowel is a should have tool. Utilize it to dig, show up the earth, or pull up persistent fallen leaves. A hand trowel is, in fact, the first garden device I purchased when we began container gardening on the outdoor patio of our home, so it is a device I commonly recommend for urban gardeners.

Hand trowels are ideal for moving dirt into pots or planting seed starting as well as bulbs. Since they're straightforward to put down and also misplace while you're working in the yard, search for hand devices with brilliant takes care of that are simple to identify in the dirt or plant.

Pruning Shears

This is an additional tool needed, no matter exactly how your yard. A lot of reducing and trimming tasks can be handled with a great pair of pruning shears. I discover them vital for collecting natural herbs, fruits, and vegetables.

They're also fantastic for cutting thick stems as well as small branches. They're especially valuable later in summer when veggie stems, as well as vines, are abundant. I additionally utilize them at the end of the season when I'm tidying up and placing the yard to bed. They're fantastic for reducing plants for the compost pile.

Garden Hand protections

You might not think of these as a device, but I locate handwear covers to be a vital thing in my tool shed. Handwear covers not only safeguard your hands from getting filthy yet likewise protecting you from injury. If you deal with thorny branches or irritable plants, gloves will undoubtedly protect your hands and wrists from square one, scrapes, and also splinters.

If you have sensitive skin as I do after that gardening, handwear covers aren't optional. I need to put on handwear covers in the garden to prevent breakouts as well as allergic reactions to plants, plant foods, and also other chemicals. Eczema prone garden enthusiasts need a good set of handwear covers to protect their hands. They also make touchscreen garden handwear covers now, which are best if you pay attention to songs or podcasts on a smart device while you garden.

Rake

Rakes are indispensable tools for any person with a yard. While fallen leave rakes can be utilized for a selection of objectives, a bow rake is excellent to use in the garden. A bow rake can be used to clear leaves or spread compost. It's also excellent for leveling soil or breaking up hard yard dust in the spring.

When we initially transitioned from container horticulture on a patio to an elevated bed neighborhood yard, we assumed we could just manage with the hand tools we 'd utilized previously. When spring came, and it was time to work the dust as well as mix in garden compost, we recognized explicitly just how challenging that was with only hand devices. One more garden enthusiast offered us their bow rake to help spread our fertilizer as well as now we have our very own to utilize in the garden. This is need to have for yards, raised beds, and even area garden stories.

Digging Shovel

If you're gardening in your lawn or an increased bed, you'll discover that an excavating shovel is an incredibly valuable device. Not only can you utilize it to dig openings, but it's also additionally excellent for transporting dust from a wheelbarrow to your garden without having to unload the whole load.

Shovels are additionally great for mixing compost heap or blending potting dirt before you add it to your containers. If you require to develop a garden or degree ground, a sharp shovel is excellent for transforming dust or removing it. Try to find sharp shovels, like the one imagined, for excavating. If you discover routine shovels are also hefty, some styles are made from light-weight materials but are still ideal for digging in yards.

Garden Spade

While you might have all of your excavating needs taken care of by a hand trowel and also an excavating shovel, you may locate a yard spade to be extremely practical in your garden bed.

Designed to use in tight and rough spaces, the square-shaped blade is perfect for digging holes, especially in recognized gardens where you don't wish to disturb existing plants. I likewise enjoy them for eliminating weeds that have deep origin systems I can not pull out by hand. If you have a seasonal, you require to transplant, and a spade is ideal to "eliminate" the plant from the dust and afterward dig a brand-new hole for it. Since it's mostly like a shovel, you can likewise use it for carrying dirt and general excavating in your lawn or garden bed.

Yard Hoe

We always get a great deal of usage out of our home in the springtime when we're preparing the yard for planting. The blade is perfect for weeding, conveniently cutting through unwanted development and removing it out of your yard beds. You can additionally use it to spread out compost in tight spaces.

The type of hoe and also the shapes and size of the blade will indeed be identified by the kind of horticulture you do. If you're handling significant areas of dirt or vegetable gardens, you might require a bigger hoe. For blossom yards, a delicate blade might work much better.

Select a Blade width based upon your needs; you may also want to get several hoes of various sizes to deal with a more significant range of tasks.

Tube + Spray Nozzles

Unless every one of your plants is in self-watering containers, you're going to need to sprinkle your garden. While some city garden enthusiasts can get away with merely a watering can, if you have a lawn, then a garden hose will be the most effective method to water your plants. While conventional pipes are still very typical, we recommend a light-weight growable tube that is less complicated to steer. (While there's a lot of brand names available, check out our testimonial of the Pocket Hose pipe for more information about these growing hose pipes.).

In addition to a hose, make sure you get an adjustable spray nozzle. These not only help you control the water, so you aren't squandering any type of water between your garden beds. Yet, they additionally assist you in managing the way the water is provided. Many spray nozzles have flexible spray patterns, permitting you to mist freshly planted seeds and seedlings while saturating well-known plants like tomatoes or blossom bushes that need great deals of water in the heat of summertime.

Wheelbarrow.

If you're lucky sufficient to have a beautiful colossal backyard to garden in, you'll find that a wheelbarrow or a garden cart will undoubtedly make a lot of tasks so much easier. Move dust, compost, even piles of fallen leaves quickly throughout your property. They're also fantastic for moving new seed startings to your garden bed.

A standard wheelbarrow-style will be best if you're frequently moving soil or garden compost as it's simple to dump your load when you review your location. If you primarily require to relocate tools or plants, then a cart layout could function much better for you.

Loppers.

If you have trees or hedges that ever before need trimming, an essential pair of pruning shears will not suffice (hah!). Loppers are ideal for keeping your bushes under control or eliminating infected branches.

A beautiful pair of loppers will allow you to cut branches approximately 1-2 ″ in size. When you're going shopping, ensure to pay attention to limit thickness the loppers will cut. Typically, longer loppers can reduce thicker branches. If you can manage the extra price, buy one that can take care of 2 ″ branches.

Weeder.

Weeds are the scourge of a gardener's existence and also can be a significant pain to remove. Fortunately, there are a couple of helpful devices to make use of to battle weeds in your yard. The very first is a hand weeder (pictured), which some call a dandelion miner. It's made to help eliminate weeds with a faucet root, with the branches penetrating the dirt to pull the extract easily.

Some choose standup weeders. You press the spikes right into the ground, push down on the bar with your foot, and get hold of the weed and its origins. They're less complicated to make use of if you have back issues or a ton of dandelions to eliminate from your backyard.

Hori Garden Knife.

Occasionally described as a yard blade, the Hori come from Japan; however, it has ended up being popular with garden enthusiasts throughout the globe. It's a stainless take blade that is slightly bent with a sharp edge as well as a serrated side. That makes it ideal for puncturing dirt or roots. Some people also utilize it as a weeder.

Some people utilize a hori rather than a hand trowel, as you can quickly use it to hair transplant plants and also dig openings for planting. Lots of models additionally have dimensions etched in the blade, making it easy to gauge depth when growing seeds. Campers likewise discover a Hori beneficial for digging into hardpacked dust or prying up rocks under your outdoor tents.

Spading fork.

You may recognize a spading fork as an excavating fork, yard fork, or a group. Similar in appearance to a pitchfork, a spading bend is indicated for turning dust and soil. Generally, it has four durable tines ideal for loosening hard dust and training soil. It's also lovely to blend fresh compost into recognized beds. It's called a spading fork since there are some circumstances where it functions far better than a standard spade since it's best for raking out weeds or breaking up globs of dust in limited rooms in already established gardens.

Readily available in full size or handheld models, choose one that works best for the size of your garden. Container gardeners will undoubtedly do merely fabulous with a portable spading fork. Yet, those with increased beds or traditional garden beds may locate a full-size tool that will work best.

Pruning SawIf, you have branches as well thick for your lopper to cut; after that, a pruning saw is a device you require. These devices are the middle ground in between a lopper and a handsaw or chain saw. The one trimming saw photos can cut through branches of to 8 inches thick, perfect for pruning trees in your backyard. You can likewise use it for shrubs and also plants.

If you're trying to minimize the variety of yard tools you have, I 'd advise getting a good set of pruning shears, and also a trimming saw as well as just avoid the loppers. While you might need to take care of the majority of your branch reducing requirements with your handsaw, the style of trimming saws is best for slicing off limbs in limited spaces, particularly when taking care of little trees and also bushes.

Lawn edger.

As you might presume from the name, an edger is meant to develop edges in your yard. A lawn edger is made use of to cut a clean line in the soil between lawn and a pathway, driveway, or a yard bed. They're usually created in a fifty percent circle form with a lip on the leading where you can push the device down with your foot. To use the tool, you position the blade where you wish to produce the edge and, after that, step down to cut into the soil and rock the lawn edger side to side before moving to repeat the steps.

A lawn edger is a specific tool that doesn't have a lot of uses, yet if you wish to produce specified lines in your backyard, it's the perfect way to separate the lawn from your yard. The developed lines will certainly make your garden and paths look neat as well as well planned.

TECHNIQUES FOR GARDENING

1. Make Compost

It's effortless to fall into assuming that garden compost's last name is a container, which careful layering and also turning are part of the deal. However, loading shredded leaves behind-the-scenes counts even. So does "trench composting," convenient for those with little yard space, therefore does bring your kitchen area scraps to a location (try the closest community yard) that will compost them if you can not. I have a pal in Manhattan, for instance, who brings her coffee premises, orange peels as well as such to the Lower East Side Ecology Facility at Union Square Greenmarket.

2. Usage Compost

Spread it around plants to fend off condition; put a bit in your potting mix to add slow-release trace elements; top-dress beds with it to improve soil framework regardless of what sort of dirt you have; utilize it to assist restore life to earth that's worn down from years of chemical abuse. Sprinkle it on the grass spring as well as fall to encourage the shallow lawn origins ... It's almost impossible to use way too much.

3. Plant Crops in Wide Beds

Crops are anything grown for the gathering: veggies, reducing flowers, bushes on hold to be transplanted ... keeping these organized as firmly as possible in beds that are not walked upon lower weeding, conserves water, allows it to be concentrated where it will certainly do the most excellent as well as enhances dirt framework year upon year as the layers of raw material accumulate. These beds are frequently increased or at the very least confined neatly by boards or-- I saw it as soon as and also am still satisfied all these years later-- by lengthy pieces of granite. Appearances aside, the essential virtue of this cleanliness is more straightforward course upkeep. From the dirt and also plant point of view, it's the unique treatment that matters.

4. Compost

Compost garments the dirt in a safety obstacle that moderates temperature, conserves water, assists maintain soil-borne diseases from sprinkling up and also helps keep dirt itself from splashing up-- on your lettuce, as an example. Almost any type of organic mulch that will certainly rot down into the soil is generally more useful to landscape material with some sort of icing, yet choosing the right mulch for each work is worth the added initiative.

Straw, for instance, is low-cost. However, it's untidy compared to timber chips, and it breaks down a whole lot faster. That suits straw to the veggie patch while the chips win under shrubs. (The specialized composts for heating soil and mirroring back directly the appropriate light upon your veggies are seldom eco-friendly. My trying outs they are ongoing, so all I can say at this point is: Remember that they function only when light falls on them; a lot more your yard appears like a forest-- no names, please-- the less efficient they will be.).

5. Feed the Soil, Not the Plant kingdoms.

Short version: Processed food, including natural junk food, has lots of calories as well as might include added vitamins. However, it's not incredible, long-lasting nutrition, for many factors we've learned as well as others we can up until now only observe. Our bodies understand the difference between consuming a carrot and taking a pill of vitamin A. Exact the same handle the soil.

More extended version: Plant health depends upon healthy and balanced roots; healthy roots rely on healthy soil for air, water, and also nutrients delivered in kinds plants can make use of. Dirt abundant in raw material-- compost!-- is typically rich in nutrients and in the bursting life (fungi's, germs, worms, and so on) that makes those nutrients readily available to the plants.

Decorative plants in high soil rarely need added plant food, and crop plants that do require extra food need less, when it's launched gradually by friendly earth from points like rock powders, kelp as well as eco-friendly manures. For an instance of just how this deals with nitrogen, of one of the essential nutrients, here's a Rodale Institute Research Study Report.

6. Share Something.

If you've obtained a yard, you're rich. Got seeds? The Seed Savers Exchange isn't nearly veggies; there's an associated Blossom as well as Natural herb exchange, as well. Got flowers? Hospitals won't take them any longer

(allergies), yet group residences, soup kitchens and also-
- why not?-- your neighborhood equipment store may be
delighted with a little bit of brightening up. Got create?
There are a national umbrella advocate vegetable
gardeners that want to grow a row for the starving, and
also lots of food banks, farmers' markets, and also
community gardens have established organized
contributions. However, no legislation states you can not
just provide your new beans to any individual that
genuinely desires them. Cravings aren't always physical.

The garden itself is worth sharing as well. Yard tours
are prominent fundraising events, so if you're up for the
consequent stress, it's most likely there's a reason that's
searching for areas. In my experience with these points,
there's always a great deal even more preparation than I
have allowed for ... yet also a great deal more repaid in
brand-new good friends, originalities as well as billions
of pats.

7. Be There.

Whether Lao-Tse said it or otherwise, it's true: The
very best plant food is the shadow of the garden
enthusiast.

WHY IS GARDENING IMPORTANT?

O ur environment is experiencing a tough circumstance as well as we, the entire human race is significantly responsible for this. We are ruining our atmosphere consciously or subconsciously without even realizing its consequences. Now we need to act really smart and also strategy something to sustain what we still have. We have to think of our future generation as well so that they get all the required assistance from nature to lead healthy and balanced lives. To do so, we require to make use of 100% natural services very wisely.

Horticulture is continuously an excellent as well as pleasant atmosphere idea as well as if you can go with sustainable horticulture after that it will undoubtedly be even more useful for all. Growing your food is excellent, always aids. Gardening is a preferred leisure activity for many. It is the moment to guide your hobby in the direction of a much more meaningful intention. No matter if you are a novice, you can start thinking about sustainable gardening. Regardless of how little your effort is, sustainable methods have significant influence. We are trying to environment-friendly nowadays to secure our setting. There are numerous various other small things that we can do to add. You need not make a lot of changes in your life if you choose gardening with lasting measures. A little effort from your side can do the technique.

What is sustainability: Sustainability is a means to keep or to withstand natural deposits that we need to survive. Nature has many things to offer us, yet mistreating those resources can be dangerous for us and also our future generation. We have been misusing natural deposits because of a very long time now. So now we need to beware and also need to utilize these resources carefully so that we proceed using them always without any shortage. To make this photo more transparent, we can take among the primary natural resource right into factor to consider, which is water. Water deficiency is a typical issue which we can attend to by utilizing sustainable procedures. Water deficiency is not only single trouble, but it is having many more heavy impacts connected with it. Sustainability is utilizing water and all other natural deposits in an organized way to reduce their misuse and to save and shield them as much as feasible so that we can use them for life.

Sustainable gardening: When we usually do gardening, we need to utilize a few active ingredients to grow plants. Several of them are natural deposits like water, landscape, soil, sunlight, and also many points such as this. Utilizing these sources, smartly belongs to sustainable horticulture. In this manner, we can make it a lot more healthy as well as environment-friendly. Now there are a couple of methods that you can utilize for sustainable gardening. This is very basic. We can use much less water and also can make use of organic things to grow plants too. These are the fundamental sustainable measures. To do so, we need to have appropriate knowledge regarding horticulture and its need so that we can utilize proper sources without wasting any one of them. To do so, we can look into the plants we wish to grow. Just then, we can utilize the correct amount of water as well as can create the landscape according to need. Here are a couple of steps:

- Oscillating Lawn sprinklers are not a fantastic choice always. You can utilize soaker hoses to ensure that you do not lose any water.

- You can try to keep water so that you can use them for horticulture. Rainwater harvesting is a fantastic lasting action.

- Try usage less power-driven tools for horticulture, as well as if you utilize any like a mower, try to have it serviced regularly.

- Prevent utilizing plastics in any type of kind while gardening. Plastics are harmful to us and also for our setting.

- Select your plants wisely if you have a lower area after that, pick your plants as necessary.

- You can reuse the fallen leaves from your yard to compost them.

- Do not use the waste from your yard for landfilling. Instead, send them for reusing your neighborhood waste reusing program.

In today's active life, we do not obtain much time to enter tune with our environment. Horticulture allows us to do so. It aids in developing a healthier environment also. From producing oxygen to produce some even more plant, gardening always helps. We likewise can have some pesticide-free, fresh food if we grow them in our yard. This way, there are numerous benefits to horticulture. This is a terrific method to work out in addition to nature and enjoy its fruits for a very long time. It is not that we need a big area to start horticulture. There are various procedures to do it, making use of minimum rooms as well. We can do it in our balcony or pots on the terrace in our apartments. So you do not have several reasons to hesitate this moment. This is the right time to act as well as do some good to shield our very own environment, and also horticulture is just one of the most natural methods.

6 TRICK IMPORTANCE OF BACKYARD GARDENS

1. Resource of fresh as well as organic food.

Who wouldn't select fresh as well as organic food?. Residence yards are incredibly manageable, and also typically, in cases of pests and even condition control, natural methods might easily be applied. It is incredibly crucial when you are very sure as well as have complete control over the top quality of food created. You can not be so confident of what is around. Make use of that.

2. Gardening is a very good physical as well as a mental exercise.

The professional's state, gardening tasks like dirt prep work, planting, removal of weeds, watering, and so on involve most of your muscular body tissues and are excellent exercises. Horticulture involves your mind as well. They say, gardening 45 mins mornings each day before any other job, prepares you literally and psychologically like thirty minutes of aerobics.

3. Supplements family budgets.

In our area, several families' (usually huge) expenditure on food is greatly minimized. These are households that proactively grow home gardens, and also they can cut down spending on food to around 40%. Adding to this, they ensure the top quality of the fruit and vegetables. This has been a significant motivation for lots of to plant home gardens in many families. Some households just need to acquire cooking oil as well as flavors, and et cetera comes from their gardens.

4. Year-round food schedule from yards.

Because yards are relatively tiny in land size, irrigation is much more comfortable and so continuous food supply through the seasons. Try it.

5. Horticulture makes good use of the room as well as protects the soil.

Placing it in this manner, we make use of the soil space around your house to grow a yard that offers all the advantages mentioned over and also the one listed below. Plus, when we cover the soil with valuable cover plants, disintegration is decreased, and even regular bush growth around your house is minimized. I hope we have made that point more clear.

6. Home entertainment, fulfillment as well as imagination.

The one having the experience can well clarify this point. It is a good feeling. Try it. Gardening is a source of entertainment and draws out lots of creativity in you. The art of planting various crops in the dirt, nurturing them as well as enjoying them grow by the day and also finally so see them blossom right into fruits is such a good feeling. You would be proud to state at the table, "this food is from my yard." So fulfilled.

HOW DO YOU START A
GARDEN?

Followings are some basic steps to start gardening.

Decide first What You would like to grow in Your Home Garden.

If you do not consume a plant, don't grow it in your vegetable garden. (I break this regulation for flowers. Edible or not, I such as to see a minimum of a few in every Garden.) Concentrate on the fruits, vegetables, or herbs that your family enjoys the most. Ensure your leading options make sense for your area. Determine your gardening area as well as estimated first and last frost days. Ideally, talk to active gardeners in your area to figure out which crops grow well and which do not.

In my north yard, plants that take control of 100 days to mature or high temps are a wager. As an example, we appreciate watermelons, yet I stick to selections like Blacktail Hill (70 days) instead of Carolina Cross (90 days). My southern gardening pal, Brownish-yellow, has difficulties with plants like peas, which favor cooler temperatures, as well as creeping plant crops like cucumbers, which are prone to mildew in high humidity. If you just desire a small garden, do not attempt to grow something like a giant pumpkin, which will top a considerable area.

Pick a Place to Begin Your Garden

Most fruits and vegetables require full sunlight, with a minimum of 5 hrs of straight sunlight per day for fruiting. Environment-friendlies, herbs, and root veggies will grow in partial shade. Southern yards may gain from late afternoon color, whereas north gardens likely require all the sunlight they can obtain.

Think of exactly how you will certainly access the yard for choosing, watering, and caring for your plants. Out of site usually equates to out of mind-- as well as an overlooked garden. Prevent high wind locations and also frost pockets (reduced areas where frost is likely to resolve).

Keep an eye out for wildlife, family pet damages as well as children's backyard. When we initially moved here, our next-door neighbor's dog would arbitrarily visit as well as dash with the Garden. This was tough on new seedlings. Now the dog is gone, but the deer, as well as wild bunnies, involve check out, so we prepare as necessary.

Plan Your Garden Beds

Once you understand where you want your yard, pick the type as well as the size of the garden bed(s). Raised beds are appealing and may make it easier to operate in your yard, but they also dry quicker. In arid locations, sunken beds can be utilized to collect offered dampness.

Think of growing your yard in blocks or beds of plants instead of single rows. Mattresses should be 3 to 4 feet throughout-- slim enough that you can reach the center from either side. Beds need to be approximately 10 feet long or less, so you're not attracted to enter the mattress as well as portable the ground.

Within the yard beds, area plants in rows or a grid pattern. The objective is to minimize walkways as well as optimize growing space. You just include fertilizer and also dirt changes to the growing area, which saves time and money. Collaborate with buddy plants to attract beneficial bugs and also enhance returns.

Beginning tiny, and make sure to offer each plant enough area to grow. The seeds and also transplants are small. However, full-grown plants can get big. Chock-full plants have difficulty swelling. A small, well-tended yard can generate as much or more than a big, inadequately had a tendency garden.

Rectangle-shaped or square beds are one of the most typical. However, you're only restricted by your creativity and also building skills. Most elevated bed packages are rectangle-shaped, yet you can also grow your yard in located products like old livestock water storage tanks or sections of drain pipeline.

Upright Horticulture

If you grow vertically, you can press even more crops right into much less room. The very best publication I've found today on the topic is "Just how to Grow Even More Veggies, (as well as Fruits, Nuts, Berries, Grains, and Other Plants) Than You Ever Before Thought Feasible on Less Land Than You Can Visualize."

I trellis/fence or otherwise grow up and down my tomatoes, beans, peas, cucumbers, and also periodically various other plants. Look into 10 Factors to Garden Up Instead of Out for even more details.

What if you have a backyard with a restricted growing area? Consider grow containers to start your Garden. Self-watering boxes are a lot more forgiving than terracotta flower pots, which tend to dry promptly.

Buy Basic Yard Tools

The right tools make operating in your yard a satisfaction as opposed to a chore. You do not make use of a butter blade to cut up raw carrots, and you shouldn't make use of dull or lightweight devices to operate in your yard. Fundamental gardening tools consist of:

- Garden hoe

- Scuffle hoe

- Dust rake

- Fallen leave rake

- Yard Shovel or D take care of Shovel

- Hand devices

Don't buy cheap plastic tools. Shop backyard as well as estate sales for bargains on genuine metal devices, or see your regional garden center. Get accessories that are the best dimension for you to decrease the threat of injury. Suitable devices will save time and effort, and your back. Keep devices tidy and also sharp, just like you ought to treat an excellent blade. To find out exactly how to maintain your appliances in good condition, go to "Cleansing and also Sharpening Yard Equipment."

Test Your Soil

Before you begin building your garden beds or planting, you need to recognize something regarding your yard dirt. Is your soil acidic, basic, or neutral pH? Do you have sand, silt, rocks, or a mix of all? Exists a threat of dirt contamination from nearby frameworks, highways, or various other sources? Does it have the right quantity of essential nutrients?

Some of these features can be figured out only by checking out the soil. Others might need residence examinations or special laboratory tests. For example, lead contamination from old home paint or nearby highways with the rush hour is an issue in some locations.

Most garden plants like dirt with a pH around 7 (neutral), although some like conditions that are somewhat acidic (potatoes, for example) or slightly alkaline (brassicas). Well, balanced nutrient levels are likewise crucial, as is the presence of raw material.

Build Your Dirt

If you're starting with turf, you'll either require to cut it up in pieces and also repurpose it, till it in or lay down damp paper or cardboard to smother it and also build a bed on top. Preparing in autumn is best, yet don't allow that stop you from starting in spring. Many plants like a deep, well-drained, abundant soil abundant in organic matter. Plant origins require excellent yard soil to produce unique vegetables and also fruit. When you start a yard, you'll gain a brand-new admiration for healthy soil as it boosts year after year. Healthy, vivid soil = healthy, vibrant plants with integrated with illness as well as parasite resistance and also even more nutrition.

TIPS TO MAXIMIZE YOUR HARVEST

If your yard is a productive one and not just a landscaping initiative for aesthetic allure, you want it to be as efficient as well as useful as feasible. It can be much harder than it wants to enhance return and obtain a far better harvest; however, we've got a few tips to aid you to work smarter as well as to get more out of your Garden. Below are seven wise means to enhance your Harvest:

1. Extend your growing period. To generate more, you require a longer growing period. Indeed, you're restricted by your environment, yet only to a specific extent. Even if you can't manage a greenhouse, you can begin previously with interior seed startings or by utilizing cloches as well as cold frames. Go further in the fall with conservatories as well as row covers along with by doing 2nd plantings of cold-weather plants, like lettuce.

Know Your Yard's Microclimate

Many environment maps cover locations that are also wide to be valuable for any details garden. The latest USDA map is much better than the old one yet still isn't genuinely exact. The only way to recognize your yard's microclimate is to maintain your records throughout the years. However, because the weather is never the same two years in a row, also your very own records will, at best, supply averages.

Not only does the climate modification from year to year, but mini locations within your Garden might vary dramatically from each other. Becomes part of your yard shaded by trees or buildings? Is some area shielded from the fresh or drying wind by a fence or bushes? Exist reduced places where chilly air and frost readily settle?

Select vegetables called growing best in your primary environment. If your Garden has greater than one microclimate, try different ranges in different areas. Some may do better than others in particular places; some may do better one year than in the next.

Plant Usually

Continuous growth is the most effective means to stretch the Harvest over an amount of time. One successive growing method is to sow seeds and laid out concurrently began seed startings of the same range.

One more succeeding planting approach is to replant at periodic periods. Sow radishes and spinach once a week; plant beans, beets, carrots, scallions, and salad greens every two weeks; plant cucumbers and also summer season squash as soon as a month. Given that you can't inform ahead of time just how warm or cool down the season will be maintain growing till seeds stop sprouting well.

A 3rd method for ensuring a succeeding harvest is to plant seeds of several various selections that grow at different rates. Growing rows of different varieties is a straightforward method to grow the Harvest of corn and also peas. For carrots, radishes, as well as salad greens, you have the alternative of mixing the seeds of various varieties and planting them done in the same row.

In our yard, we obtain the best selection of salad eco-friendlies over the lengthiest amount of time by both different mixing types of lettuce seed together and growing the mix every two weeks. We do the very same with radishes. When our weather condition all of a sudden transforms warm (as it does annually), some selections will undoubtedly run for cover. In contrast, others continue supplying us with fresh salads for a couple of weeks, much longer.

Continue succeeding growing as the weather warms, replacing spring crops with summertime plants and also summer crops with fall veggies. Besides extending the Harvest, successive growing has an added benefit-- it maintains the dirt active as well as thereby prevents weeds.

Hit Weeds Early and also Hard

Veggies grow fastest and also create the highest yields if they don't need to compete with weeds. Yet any time you function the dirt, you motivate weeds to grow. As quickly as you see plants growing along your recently growed rows, hoe them down. Repeat in two weeks, as well as once more two weeks later. Afterward, you ought to have no more than the occasional weed, particularly if you tuck veggies into a thick layer of compost as they grow.

2. Garden compost, garden compost, garden compost. Make your very own compost from the cooking area as well as lawn waste, and also you will certainly make sure to grow even more as well as harvest extra. The nutrients included in the soil from the compost will increase your returns.

Garden compost is abundant in nutrients. It is made use of, for example, in yards, landscape design, cultivation, urban agriculture, and also natural farming. The garden compost itself is beneficial for the land in many ways, including as a soil conditioner, a fertilizer, enhancement of vital humus or humic acids, and also as an all-natural chemical for soil. In communities, compost is useful for disintegration control, land and also stream reclamation, wetland building, and as landfill cover.

At the most comfortable degree, the procedure of composting requires making a lot of wet organic matter, such as leaves, lawn, as well as food scraps, and waiting for the materials to break down right into humus after months. Nonetheless, composting can also happen as a multi-step, very closely monitored process with determining inputs of water, air, as well as carbon- and also nitrogen-rich materials. The decomposition process is assisted by shredding the plant matter, including pool, as well as making sure correct aeration by frequently turning the mixture when open stacks or "windrows" are utilized. Fungus, earthworms, and also various other detritivores further separate the product. Bacteria needing oxygen to work and also mushrooms take care of the chemical procedure by converting the inputs into warm, CO_2, and ammonium.

3. Method sequence growing. Use the very same area for greater than one plant. When an early period crop is done, put in a warm-weather vegetable. After that, plant new cold-weather plants in the autumn. You can additionally plant the same thing in succession, re-seeding after one collection of plants has run out.

Four standard techniques can also be combined.

- Two or even more plants in succession: After one plant is collected, another is planted in the very same area. The length the growing season, climate, and also crop selection are essential elements. As an example, a fantastic season springtime crop could be followed by a heat-loving summer plant.

- **Same crop, successive growing:** Several smaller sized plantings are made at timed intervals, instead of at one time. The plants grow at staggered days, developing a constant harvest over an extended duration. Lettuce and also various other salad eco-friendlies prevail plants for this method. Within a little yard or residence garden, this approach works in preventing the first large yield from the plant and also instead of giving a constant, smaller return that may be eaten in its entirety. This is likewise referred to as relay growing.

- **Two or even more plants all at once:** Non-competing plants, frequently with various maturity days, are grown together in different patterns. Intercropping is one pattern method; companion planting is an associated, complementary method. This technique is additionally referred to as Interplanting: The purpose of growing two kinds of plants in the same space.

- Interplanting requires a specific amount of preplanning and also knowledge of the maturity dates of different sorts of vegetables. It has been kept in mind that successful interplanting and too extensive horticulture is performed in increased beds within the growing areas. Planting two or more non-competing crops might increase problems with soil-borne illness and also bugs that just influence one sort of plant. Depending on exactly how close the interplanting ranges are, crop failure is an opportunity.

- **Very same crop, various maturation dates:** Numerous fields are picked, with different maturation days: early, the first period, late. Planted at the same time, the varieties grow one after the other over the season.

4. Grow up and down. Whenever possible, beginning growing plants up to obtain more out of your yard's area. Any kind of plant that has a vining nature can be educated upwards with a trellis or other framework. Not just does this get you a lot more for your room, it assists avoid fungal infections.

5. Choose high-yield plants. When you pick plants that generally generate a whole lot, you get even more Harvest with much less work. Think tomatoes, squash, lettuce and environment-friendlies, peas, and also beans.

6. Trim attentively. Don't allow your plants to run rampant. Trimming and pinching in a calculated way will undoubtedly maintain them healthy and balanced and also result in a higher yield. When you squeeze off added foliage, your plant places extra energy right into making fruits.

7. Motivate to do their thing. The much more energetic bees in your yard, the much better it is for return, thanks to pollination. Include native, flowering plants in your blossom beds and also reduce chemical usage, and the bees will help make your garden a lot more productive.

WHAT YOU CAN GROW IN YOUR GARDEN

A perfectly ripe, succulent tomato, still warm from the sunlight. Beautiful carrots, pulled from the garden minutes (or perhaps secs!) before they're consumed. Growing your very own vegetables is one of those tasks that balance usefulness and indulgence. Along with the benefit of having the fixings for a salad or light supper right outside your door, when you grow your very own vegetables, you're getting the most nutritional value as well. Plants start losing nutrients as quickly as they're collected, and top quality diminishes as sugars are developed into starches.

1. Broccoli

It is high in calcium, iron, and magnesium, along with vitamins A, B6 as well as C. In fact, one mug of raw broccoli florets gives 130 percent of your day-to-day vitamin C demand.

How to grow broccoli

- Grow it in containers: One broccoli plant per pot, pots must be 12 to 16 inches deep.

- What to look out for Cabbage worm. If you start seeing pretty white butterflies trembling around your broccoli, you're guaranteed to begin seeing little green worms throughout your broccoli plants. To avoid this, cover your plants with floating row cover or lightweight bed sheets. If you start seeing cabbage worms, just select them by hand.

2. Peas

There is nothing like plants grown right in your very own yard-- the tender sweet taste of a breeze pea simply tweezed from the vine differs anything you can acquire in at a shop. Aside from being tasty, peas are high in fiber, iron, magnesium, potassium, and vitamins A, B6, and also C.

Just how to grow peas

- Grow peas in containers: Plant peas about 2 inches apart in a pot that is at least 10 inches deep. Provide assistance for peas to climb.

- What to look out for Hot weather. When the weather condition transforms hot, pea manufacturing will indeed practically shut down. Grow peas in early spring and also late summer/autumn, or whenever of year when temperature levels are consistently between 40 and even 85 degrees Fahrenheit.

3. Beans (particularly navy beans, great northern beans, kidney beans).

While breeze beans (green beans/wax beans) are a significant enhancement to any yard, it's the beans we grow that are genuine nutritional powerhouses. Dried out beans, in general, are high in iron, fiber, manganese, and phosphorous.

Just how to grow beans.

- Grow beans in containers: Shrub beans are your best option for growing in containers. Plant beans four inches apart in a box that is at the very least 12 inches deep.

- What to keep an eye out for Harvest at the right

time. Harvest dehydrated beans when the cases have dried on the vine. The pods should be brown, and you should have the ability to feel the hard grains inside. Covering the seeds, as well as let them sit out a few days to make sure that they're scorched before saving them in jars in a fantastic, dark, arid location.

4. Brussels sprouts.

The bane of lots of childhood years, Brussels sprouts obtain a bad rap mostly because of overcooking. When prepared right, Brussels sprouts are lovely, tender, and tasty. They additionally provide tons of fiber, magnesium, potassium and also riboflavin, as well as high levels of vitamins A, B6 as well as C.

How to grow Brussels sprouts.

- Grow them in containers: Grow one plant per 16-inch deep container.

- What to keep an eye out for Cabbage worms (see "Broccoli," above.).

5. Tomatoes.

Fresh, native tomatoes are the reason numerous gardeners enter into veggie horticulture in the first place. There's just absolutely nothing that compares to eating a flawlessly ripe tomato, still warm from the sunlight. Tomatoes are likewise beneficial for us, packing a lot of fiber, iron, magnesium, niacin, potassium, and vitamins A, B6 as well as C. They're additionally a fantastic source of the antioxidant lycopene.

How to grow tomatoes.

- Grow tomatoes in containers: Container dimensions will differ, relying on the range you're growing. If you're growing an indeterminate variety, your vessel will require to be a minimum of 18 inches deep. For determinate varieties, 12 inches is an excellent depth, and also for dwarf or "outdoor patio" kind tomatoes, 8 inches is best. One tomato plant per pot.

- What to keep an eye out for Tomato horn worm can be a trouble in many areas-- these big caterpillars should be removed by hand whenever you see them. Likewise, keep an eye out for indications of affliction, which is an actual problem in numerous parts of the UNITED STATE.

6. Red bell peppers.

They are high in potassium, riboflavin, as well as vitamins A, B6, and C. Actually, one mug of red bell pepper packs an incredible 317 percent of the advised daily allowance of vitamin C as well as 93 percent of the suggested vitamin A.

How to grow black pepper

- Grow peppers in boxes or containers: Plant one pepper plant per each 8 to 12-inch deep pot.

- What to watch out for: Aphids and also flea beetles are both the most typical insect bugs when growing peppers. While both can be managed with insecticidal soap, which is an ideal organic alternative, you can also make all-natural, self-made sprays to discourage these pests. A tomato fallen leave spray will remove aphids, and garlic/hot pepper spray works very well on a flea beetle infestation.

7. Beetroots.

Beets are a great "twofer" plant-- you can gather the beetroot origins, naturally, however, you can additionally pick and also eat the eco-friendlies. Young beet greens are delicious when added to a salad, and bigger beet greens can be sauteed as a quick side recipe or made use of the means you would certainly use other greens such as spinach. (Plus: 5 methods for beetroot greens.) Beetroot roots are very high in iron, potassium as well as vitamin C. Beet eco-friendlies are also better, as they are high in iron, calcium, magnesium, potassium, zinc, and vitamins A, B6 and even C.

How to grow beetroots.

- Grow beetroots in containers: Plant beet seeds three inches apart in a box that is 12 inches deep. Because each beetroot seed is a collection of seeds, make sure to thin the seedlings to one per group. Thinning's can be included in salads or sandwiches.

- What to watch out for: Recognizing when to gather. Beetroot roots go to their most beautiful when they are harvested small-- between one as well as two inches across. At this size, they are pleasant and also tender. More significant beets tend to be a type of woody and much less tasty.

8. Leaf amaranth.

It is a less-common vegetable that is well worth a shot in your yard. The fallen leaves have a sweet and slightly tangy taste that functions well in a selection of meals, from stir-fries and also soups to merely steaming it all on its own. As a benefit, fallen leave amaranth is one of the few heat-tolerant environment-friendlies. It will not screw in the warm of summer the way spinach and also kale are prone to. Nutritionally, fallen leave amaranth is high in calcium, iron, magnesium, phosphorous, potassium, riboflavin, zinc, and even vitamins A, B6, and also C. Everyone should be growing this!

How to grow fallen leave amaranth.

- Growing leaf amaranth in containers: Spread the small seeds over the dirt's surface in a pot that goes to the very least 8 inches deep. Gather the leaves when they are two to four inches tall. You will have the ability to get at the very least 2 or 3 harvests before you need to plant more seeds.

- What to keep an eye out for Fallen leave amaranth is reasonably very easy to grow, and also reasonably problem-free. Rarely, leaf miners can become a problem.

9. Carrots.

Carrots are at their sweetest, crunchiest finest when newly gathered from the yard. These icons of healthy consuming deserve their "good-for-you" representative. In essence, they're very high in fiber, manganese, niacin, potassium, and vitamins A, B6 as well as C. Their only disadvantage is that they do tend to be high in sugar, so if you see your carbohydrate intake, you'll wish to restrict the number of carrots you eat.

How to grow carrots.

- Grow carrots in containers: Sow carrot seeds a couple of inches apart in a pot that goes to least 12 inches deep. Search for much shorter ranges, such as Thumbelina or Danvers Fifty Percent Long.

- What to keep an eye out for Harvesting at the best dimension. Carrots go to their tastiest when gathered small. Leaving them in the ground for a long time can lead to excessively large, woody carrots. You'll also wish to make sure to maintain your carrots evenly moist, as letting the soil dry out frequently can additionally cause somewhat bitter, fibrous carrots.

10. Leafy greens.

OK, I ripped off here. I can't advise just one leafed environment-friendly since they are all perfect for us, as well as scrumptious-- kale, collards, spinach, turnip, or dandelion eco-friendlies-- exactly how can you perhaps select only one? In general, the "environment-friendly leafies" consist of high quantities of calcium, iron, potassium, as well as vitamins A, B6, and also C.

How to grow kale as well as other leafy environment-friendlies.

- Grow greens in containers: Grow one kale plant per 10-inch deep pot. Various other environment-friendlies can be grown a few plants to a bowl-- they must be planted a minimum of 4 inches apart and collected little.

- What to look out for Heat and cabbage worms. The majority of leafed eco-friendlies are cool-weather crops, so they're best grown in spring and also fall in most areas-- heat will certainly create them to screw. Besides, most of these eco-friendlies are participants of the Brassicas household, which suggests they are prone to cabbage worm invasions. Control them with the very same methods laid out in the "Broccoli" section over.

Try growing a couple of (or all!) of this nutrient-dense, delicious veggie in your garden, as well as you'll obtain double the wellness benefits: healthy food and time spent outdoors, supporting your plants.

WHAT NOT TO DO IN THE GARDEN?

I t's not too early in the winter season to begin thinking of the springtime garden. I'm still completing my preparation for my yard, yet there are some methods that I understand I won't do. These are techniques that appear in the common area but can be destructive to the yard.

1. Till

Firstly, recognize that tilling does not improve the soil. Tilling can get rid of some weeds and also include organic matter. However, as an annual practice to enhance soil and even assistance boost dirt structure ... well, that's very ill-informed.

I see every person obtain their tillers out in the springtime or autumn, as well as I have to ask: What do you assume you are doing? Ask yourself that question this year. And if you can't offer yourself the right solution, don't do it. I do not work till unless I am entirely re-doing a garden and including raw material, and also, this is a single event, not an annual method.

2. Remove fallen leaves

I still cringe at the memory of removing leaves from shrub beds. It looked far better, so we loaded trash can filled with leaves and placed them in the waste. Fallen leaves are a beneficial asset, and putting them in the trash is an embarrassment. Leaving fall leaves on shrubs and various other yard beds can assist raise the organic matter in the dirt. It additionally reduces weeds and also supplies a host of numerous other advantages as compost.

3. Spray chemicals

I don't always prevent pesticides because I'm concerned about their adverse online reputation. Chemicals are just unneeded in my yard. I grow a wide variety of plants, which aids hinder bugs. I attempt to prevent parasites with crop turning, tracking, catch cropping, and also physical removal. As well as typically, when there is an episode, it's more reliable to get rid of the few contaminated plants than to put forth the cost as well as effort to use a pesticide.

4. Spray weeds

Splashing weeds without an idea are not sufficient. They will simply grow back. My weed control techniques are a lot more complicated, but additionally a lot more efficient. I try to determine the weeds in my yard and also establish the very best way to get rid of them (or, in many cases, eat them, utilize them, or endure them).

Mulch, hand weeding, and also substitute with preferred species is my first approach to get rid of weeds. My primary goal is to produce an environment that has no space for unwanted weeds. Competitors from healthy plants, as well as preventing bare dirt, are much better long-term weed control remedies than merely splashing.

5. Plant much more yard

The lawn is more typical than dirt in our contemporary landscapes. I do have a smaller sized patch of turf, but the majority of my Garden is not yard. I plant grass choices like clover, food production systems, and mulched blended planting beds.

My Garden is more diverse and also rather than being just a location to go outdoors and also cut yard; I have fruits, blossoms, veggies as well as herbs as well as areas to unwind and appreciate being outside. There are also lots of environmental advantages of decreasing the lawn, as well as changing it with a wider variety of plants.

6. Top bushes and even trees

I do not have a set of hedge clippers, and also I prefer not to give my trees and shrubs meatball or flat-top haircuts. It deserves it to find out exactly how to trim bushes as well as trees properly. Appropriate pruning will take less time and make the plant healthier and also extra charming And if you ever before see an arborist advertising and marketing tree topping, please run the other direction. Tree covering is not an excellent suggestion as well as will certainly cause an increased risk of branches falling as well as health problems for your tree.

WAY TO KEEP YOUR GARDEN HEALTHY

O ne of the most mystifying activities that can occur in your yard is when a plant obtains a disease. Just how did it take place? Will it spread out? Will all my plants die? Precisely how can I eliminate it? One of the most vital points to comprehend about condition avoidance is something called the disease triangular (illustration, right). The condition can only occur when three things correspond: you have a plant that can get ill (a host), a pathogen (like a fungus, bacterium, or infection) that can strike the plant, and also environmental problems (like moisture or drought) that promote the condition. If anyone of these things is absent, the illness will certainly not take place, so prevention includes knocking senseless at least one side of the triangle. Instead of waiting for a problem to pop up in your yard, think about the best defense versus condition to be a high crime. What follows are ten ways you can remove a minimum of one side of the situation triangular and maintain your plants healthily and balanced.

1. Analyze plants carefully before buying

The most convenient means to limit illness in your yard is to avoid presenting it in the first place. Obtaining a disease with a brand-new plant is not the sort of bonus that any of us desires. Among the hardest points to discover is what a healthy and balanced plant needs to look like, making it hard to understand if the one you want is sick.

It is an excellent idea to collect a couple of books, magazines, as well as magazines that show what a healthy sampling appears like. Do not take home a plant with dead spots, decomposed stems, or bugs. These problems can quickly spread to your healthy plants as well as are often hard to remove when established. Along with examining the tops of plants, always evaluate the origin quality. One does not often see clients doing this in a garden center, yet it needs to be a typical view. Place your hand on the dirt surface with the plant stem between your fingers. Delicately invert the pot as well as drink the plant losses. You might have to tap the edge of the cup against a secure surface area to loosen the origins from the pot.

Roots ought to be firm, usually white, and also spaced all over the root-ball. Dark or mushy backgrounds are not a good sign. Even when the tops appear healthy, it's just a matter of time before a decayed origin system kills a plant.

2. Use completely composted lawn waste

Not all products in a compost heap decompose at the same rate. Some materials might have broken down completely to be placed in the Garden, while others have not. Extensive composting produces high temperatures for extended sizes of time, which kill any kind of microorganisms in the product. Infected plant debris that has not undertaken this procedure will reintroduce potential illness right into your Garden. If you are unsure of the conditions of your compost heap, you must stay clear of using backyard waste as compost under sensitive plants as well as avoid including possibly infected debris in your collection.

3. Keep an eye on your bugs

Insect damages to plants is a lot more than cosmetic. Infections and germs commonly can only get in a plant through some kind of opening, as well as pest damage that provides that. Some insects act as transportation for infections, spreading them from one plant to the following. Aphids are just one of the most common carriers, as well as thrips spread impatiens necrotic place infection, which has ended up being a significant problem for business manufacturers over the past decade. Aster yellows (image, right) is an illness brought by leafhoppers as well as has a massive variety of host plants. Insect strikes are an additional means to put a plant under stress, rendering it much less most likely to fend off condition.

4. Tidy up in the fall

It is continuously best to clear out the yard in the fall, even if you stay at a moderate temperature and climate. This is an effective deterrent to illness yet likewise an excellent way to regulate disease currently in your Garden.

Diseases can overwinter on dead fallen leaves and also debris and also attack the brand-new fallen leaves as they emerge in springtime. Iris leaf area, daylily fallen leave streak, and even a black area on roses are examples of illness that can be drastically reduced if the dead fallen leaves are removed each loss. If you are leaving stems as well as vegetation to create winter rate of interest, be sure to remove them before brand-new growth begins in springtime.

5. Use the appropriate plant food

You require to take care when feeding plants since way too much of any type of fertilizer can shed roots, decreasing their capability to absorb water. This, in turn, makes the plants much more susceptible to tension from the dry spell, cold, as well as warmth. Plants deprived of nutrients are smaller sized as well as can be severely influenced by leaf spots, while a more vigorous plant can battle diseases. A surplus of a particular nutrient is another means to place tension on a plant.

Obtaining a dirt examination through your local expansion company will certainly supply you with exact info on nutrient degrees in your dirt. Without it, any kind of feeding off your plants is most likely to be guesswork on your component and also might result in too much of one nutrient or not sufficient of one more.

6. Plant disease-resistant varieties

Disease-resistant plants are those that could get ill with a specific problem; however, they will battle the disease. As an example, some tomatoes are coded as "VFN resistant," which implies the tomato range is immune to the fungi Verticillium and also Fusarium and to nematodes.

If you start seeking these codes on flowers, you'll most likely be dissatisfied because condition resistance is hardly ever identified on plant tags. This does not imply that numerous blossom selections are not immune to the disease. Several climbed businesses provide plants that are immune to diseases like powdery mold as well as a black area.

Nursery staff members and fellow garden enthusiasts can aid you in identifying the very best or most free ranges of many plants. Reference books and directories might likewise list plants and selections resistant to particular diseases.

7. Trim harmed limbs at the correct time

Trimming trees and also shrubs in late wintertime is better than waiting till spring. Wounded arm or legs can come to be infected over the winter months, enabling conditions to come to be developed when the plant is inactive. Late-winter trimming stops the state from spreading to new development. Although late-winter storms can trigger further damage, it is still better to trim back a broken arm or leg than ignore it until spring is underway. Always use sharp devices to clean cuts that heal swiftly, and make sure to reduce to healthy and balanced, living tissue.

INTRODUCTION TO HYDROPONICS

Hydroponics is an approach to growing and cultivating crops without soil. Plants are grown in equal and similar rows or on trellises, similar to in a conventional yard. However, they have their origins in water instead of in dust. A lot of us confuse dirt with nutrients. The soil supplies framework, not the actual food itself, for plant origins. The food comes from various other products mixed in the soil, such as compost, broken-down plant waste, or fertilizers. Plants grown hydroponically can grow faster and much healthier than plants in the dirt since they don't need to battle soil-borne diseases; also, all the food and water they need are provided straight to their roots all the time.

Hydroponics is a technique of growing crops without dirt. Plants are grown in rows or on trellises, much like in a traditional garden, yet they have their roots in water. The majority of us perplex soil with nutrients. Dirt gives structure, not the real food itself, for plant origins. The food comes from other products mixed in the ground, such as compost, broken-down plant waste, or plant foods. Plants grown hydroponically can grow faster and much healthier than plants in the dirt because they do not need to deal with soil-borne conditions; on top of that, all the food, as well as the water they require, are provided directly to their roots all the time.

Growing plants through this method do not have to be done on a large scale, and it's less complicated than you may believe. Now there are kits, DIY systems, and also even totally automated growing tables, all made for house garden enthusiasts.

Hydroponics is very easy in lots of methods; it's simpler than growing plants in dirt. Plants need food, air, and water. When you break it down, it comes to be simple to provide plants only what they need. It is the science/method of growing plants without soil. The plants prosper on the nutrient service alone; the tool simply acts as an assistant for the plants and their root systems.

As mentioned above, the process is handled, not merely regulated. Consequently, it is water efficient as well as nutrient effective, both of which are delivered straight to the plant's root structure. Since the levels of water and nutrients are checked, these components are supplied as and when required at the required degrees. Together, water and nutrients add to the success of and rate of growth.

The lighting aspect is additionally essential in crop production. This is achieved by planting out in vertical frameworks where lighting is maximized while plant thickness, crowding, and also shielding are lessened. Present-day hydroponic farming embraces the 3-D approach and are grown vertically in multilevel growing beds.

So currently, we have perfect growing conditions in terms of nutrients, water, and also light, plus the ability to grow in the upright. This includes substantially to the return each location as the growing area is no more 2-dimensional (2-D); however, it has ended up being a 3-D concept as well as layout. This makes the most of the real growing location and also utilizes what can have been unutilized areas in enclosed horticulture atmospheres.

With a multi-level bed linens framework that is movable, plants can now be revealed to optimal lighting whatsoever times throughout the growing duration. This regulated as well as handled growing environment likewise has considerable advantages over traditional farming techniques.

To begin your very own hydroponic garden, you need to determine where you will resolve your plants. The hydroponic growth of plants generally indicates that you require a respectable amount of room to allow the plants to grow. Most people use a greenhouse. The hydroponic growth of plants is rather straightforward, and also anyone can do it. All you need is to do research, particularly if you are simply starting.

Ask concerns from individuals you know who are into hydroponic horticulture. Discover what type of nutrients your plants will certainly require. Hydroponic nutrients are usually a lot more focused because of the reality that they expect to take part in the plants and their growing environment. It is best if you discover a combination solution that will certainly give all of the nutrients needed for your plants to grow.

One more benefit of hydroponic horticulture is that you can grow your vegetables and fruits throughout the year. The most optimal situation is an indoor hydroponic growing. By doing this, you can control not only the light and also water, but likewise the number of insects that will influence the yield of the plants. When growing a yard outdoors, you must be prepared to lose several of your crop yields as a result of bugs, the weather, as well as other variables. However, with hydroponic expansion, you can eliminate most of these aspects.

You can likewise make sure the number of hydroponic nutrients that your plants are obtaining. By utilizing hydroponic nutrients, you can regulate the toughness of the original systems and control the flowering power of your plants. Different types of hydroponic nutrients can enhance your plants to create more blossoms, which subsequently provide even more fruit from plants such as the tomato plant. Other sorts of hydroponic nutrients raise the size as well as foliage of the plants. Hydroponic nutrients are generally planted in food. This is as needed to the plant growth as water and light.

So currently, we understand that there go to the very least three things that are vital to hydroponic gardening: light, water, and hydroponic nutrients. Without these three things, your hydroponic yard will undoubtedly stop working. Find out about the basics of hydroponic growing to ensure a fantastic all year yard. You will not regret it when you see the bountiful harvest at the end of the roadway.

Dirt is not made use of in the growing process whatsoever, that makes is a prominent selection for gardening, as it entails extra efficiency and a minimized danger of chemicals and also various other plant bore illness. Going a step additionally, individuals have begun using natural hydroponic gardening to grow good things like vegetables and fruits.

This may come as a tragedy to the people who had never connected organic plant growing with it; yet if you think about it, the main ingredients used in hydroponics are either currently organic (water), or can be made natural (the nutrients and also plant food). So it is possible to pursue natural hydroponic gardening.

Much more about Hydroponics

The term originates from the Greek language (hydro, meaning water as well as ponos meaning labor). As mentioned over, it is a means of cultivating plants, utilizing water combined with nutrients and also growing media such as perlite, gravel, and even mineral wool. No soil is needed because dirt just works as a nutrition storage tank. It is adequate, consequently, to provide the nutrient solution to the plant origins synthetically. It is proved to be a fascinating development in the location of interior horticulture. The main reasons why plant farmers have embraced hydroponics relate mainly to cost efficiency and efficiency.

Benefits of hydroponics

- No dirt is required

- There is steady as well as considerable plant yield

- The danger of pests, as well as conditions, is considerably lowered

- The cost of water is significantly reduced since generally the water can be recycled There is much less area, growing time, as well as labor included

- The value of nutrition additionally shows to

below, since the nutrients mixed with water are recyclable

- There is virtually no nutrition air pollution owing to the reality that hydroponics is a coordinated approach of plant cultivation and can be operated in a sheltered area, utilizing artificial lighting.

WHY HYDROPONICS?

Growing food without dirt, earthworms, and, often, sunshine may go against usual suggestions of were healthy and balanced diet comes from. However, hydroponics has obliterated factor. It provides many benefits over standard soil approaches, and it may also aid resolve some of the world's growing problems.

Water Conservation

Agriculture presently uses 80 percent of the freshwater consumed in the UNITED STATE as well as 60 percent of it worldwide. On the other hand, a water scarcity crisis currently torments every continent, especially deserts such as the American West.

With a name like hydroponics, it seems without soil procedure would undoubtedly use a lot of water. Nonetheless, generally, hydroponic systems use ten times much less water than soil farming since they recirculate liquids and also reduce waste. In the hope that soilless agriculture will assist avoid around the world water wars in the following century, the National Nuclear Security Agency built a hydroponics greenhouse in New Mexico's Sandia Lab to examine the suitability of growing forage plants for animals with hydroponics.

Land Conservation

Water is not the only source in short supply. Many nations, including Terrific Britain, might encounter a substantial scarcity of farmland in the following 20 years. Some research studies approximate crop yield have to double by 2050 to meet projected demands, and also researchers caution that will certainly not occur if existing patterns continue. In the past, we've cleared forests and even grasslands to plant crops, with severe environmental consequences. What happens if there are a much better means?

Some futurists, consisting of microbiologist Dickson Despommier, are convinced hydroponics is the response. In soilless systems, roots do not need to stretch out as a lot since they're provided with all the nutrients they require. Crop yields usually are higher and also extra steady, and too artificial lighting makes year-round crops possible. It presently takes an acreage the size of Virginia to produce food for New york city City. Despommier pictures cities are feeding themselves with upright high-rise building greenhouses. "If vertical farming in metropolitan centers comes to be the standard," Despommier says, "then one anticipated lasting advantage would be the steady repair service of most of the world's harmed communities via the methodical abandonment of farmland."

Food Safety

We have actually all gotten used to headlines about deadly E.coli episodes. Twenty-three percent of foodborne illness deaths, as well as 46 percent of foodborne ailments, are connected to the eating method, according to the Center for Condition and also Prevention. Soil contaminated by livestock waste is usually pinpointed as the reason.

Since hydroponic systems are sterile and also don't have dirt to be contaminated, illness breakouts are less likely, especially in clean, well-run systems. (Nevertheless, hydroponics does not entirely remove the threat of foodborne ailment. Appropriate preventative measures are called for).

HYDROPONICS FOR THE
HOME GARDENER

The first, as well as frequently the most challenging decision for any type of gardener, is what to grow. The very best veggies to grow in any kind of garden are the ones a person or family delights in one of the most. Yet some plants tend to function better than others in tiny hydro-systems.

A herb garden is an excellent method to get started. But before diving in, it helps to comprehend the standard parts as well as six various sorts of hydroponics systems. With a little standard understanding, any individual can make a basic system. A secure wick system is the easiest to start with because it doesn't call for a pump, timer, or power. (For those not DIY-inclined, several companies use hydroponic starter sets.).

Unending Benefits

A well made hydroponic system is identified by less wastage of water as well as nutrients than soil-based farms. Both water and also nutrients are feed straight to the root structure of the plants as well as recycled with the hydroponic system. This likewise gets rid of the typical land as well as water contamination opportunities due to overland flow as well as runoff, correctly.

This all means the system makes use of much less water as well as much fewer nutrient supplies. Both of these aspects give fantastic economic benefits by decreasing the continuous costs of farming, therefore, leading the way for sustainable agriculture. This is of vital importance in areas placed as having severe scarcity of water.

In the absence of the soil medium, the likelihood of disease is significantly reduced. This is an additional plus variable. Conventional farming approaches are dirt based. The job strength if earth-based farming is very various to hydroponic technique. Standard farming includes the tilling as well as the cultivation of the soil. Both of these activities are time-consuming and labor-intensive before the growing period. Other plus variables of hydroponics are the administration of the thickness of plants and also the moisture of the growing atmosphere.

As these variables are all handled, there is no requirement for airing out of the plant crop nor for weeding. There are no microorganisms as there is no dirt stratum. There is no fallen leave consuming predators as a result of the handled units. Therefore, hydroponics is ending up being the agrarian farmer's dream. In other words, the nature of the farming workload is substantially minimized in comparison to the standard farming techniques.

WHAT IS ORGANIC HYDROPONIC GARDENING?

The word organic is made use of to define anything that originates from the earth, like plants, pets, and vegetables. Organic Horticulture hence indicates that no synthetically developed active ingredients are used in the plant growing process. As it is the corner stones in hydroponics, water, is organic, and organic plant food can likewise be originated from cows, chicken, algae, sheep manure, bones, and also other many other all-natural resources.

It may be worth keeping in mind here that together with the water mixed nutrients, plants additionally require air and also nitrogen to grow and even succeed well. Also, there likewise needs to an appropriate content of pH (potential Hydrogen) in the plant food. It is a tried and tested fact that hydroponics conducted with an organic plant food along with various other natural horticulture procedures, it leads to more productive, better plants returns.

A remarkable advantage of organic hydroponics is that one can derive the combined outcomes that originate from dirt based on hydroponic gardening. This helps to do away with the inconvenience of developing the best mix of chemicals, which, if generally refrained, brings about plant damage.

HYDROPONICS TECHNIQUES

Hydroponics was initially defined as "the growing of plants in water," however, with the effective use of the method for cultivating plants in the air as well as other media besides water, the interpretation was transformed to the much more comprehensive - "the cultivation of plants without soil." Hydroponic strategies have shown efficiency for industrial farming and also in house gardening. Hydroponic techniques and also systems have substantially benefited farming, especially where standard soil cultivation is not feasible as a result of the absence of agricultural land, sources, or various other elements.

Hydroponic Systems and Techniques

The scientific research of hydroponics has advanced since its inception with the development of two major systems - the water-based hydroponic systems and accumulation based hydroponic systems. Water-based hydroponic systems utilize water around the plant to favor the distribution of nutrients. In accumulated based systems, plant origins are supported in some kind of inert product such as Rockwool, pebbles, and so on. Both Water Culture Hydroponic Equipment and Accumulation based Hydroponic Solutions may make use of numerous various techniques of nutrient shipment to plant roots depending upon demands specific to the system.

Basic Methods Of Hydroponics

All hydroponics systems work with the same concept: plants grow in a clean and sterile, soil-less tool that allows the distribution of nutrients to the roots straight from nutrient-enriched water service. These systems differ mainly in structure. Each of the following six methods utilizes a unique technique to provide nutrients to the growing plants.

Wick

Equally, as the name implies, this system utilizes one or several wicks to draw nutrient service from a reservoir right into a sterile medium such as perlite, vermiculite, or Rockwool. A wick system is cheap and also straightforward to set up and does not call for any kind of pumps or fancy water drainage systems.

Plants grow straight in the medium and also occupy the nutrients as needed. These systems are perfect for tiny sets up, such as an interior kitchen area garden or collection of home plants. It is not, nevertheless, the most efficient distribution system as well as may not have the ability to appropriately stay on par with the demands of big or swiftly growing plants.

Drip

A drip system uses a complicated system of hoses and drip lines to take vitamins and mineral remedies to each specific plant. Each plant is usually rooted in a relatively reliable tool, such as Rockwool cubes, to stop obstructing lines. This sort of system works well for bigger plants, such as tomatoes, that requirement to grow for an extended period before harvest. The primary disadvantage of drip systems is cost and maintenance. The many drip lines, emitters, pumps, and also equipment can be excessively costly for a small pastime garden and blocked, or leaky lines are typical troubles. Cleansing this complex system can be tough as well as taxing, possibly making your enjoyable new leisure activity a lot more difficult than it's worth.

Ups and downs

An ups and downs system utilizes a timed pump to regularly flood as well as drain pipes a growing table, on which plants are rooted in a sterilized medium. The regular flooding keeps the roots moist as well as well-fed, while the drainpipe cycle ensures they can get sufficient oxygen. This system is not extremely pricey, is easy to keep, and is not vulnerable to much of the troubles connected with various other methods. While this system is straightforward and also sensible for a greenhouse setting, it doesn't lend itself well to a tiny, kitchen-counter, or sunroom garden. Tables are usually developed to be sturdy as well as useful, yet not necessarily appealing. Unlike the drip and also wick systems, it can be challenging to make an ebb and flow system instead.

Nutrient Film Technique

This system is additionally better fit to a greenhouse or more extensive operation than for an at-home job. The Nutrient Film Method (NFT) has plants suspended in plastic baskets and also sometimes little Rockwool cubes over long tubes or trays. Nutrient service flows via the cells onto the plants' origins and, after that, drains back right into the reservoir. This system supplies many advantages. Without little drip lines or timers, there are fewer elements that could create problems. Specific plants can be removed as well as replaced without disturbing the rest of the system. One prospective downside of the NFT system is that any system failure or power interruption leaves the origins at risk to rapid drying.

Water Society

Water culture is the system frequently utilized readily to produce little, water-loving, quick-growing plants like lettuce or spinach. It is usually a bit greater than a tray, constructed from Styrofoam or comparable product, floating on the storage tank. This system can be as huge or as tiny as you want and also is easily adjusted to any type of variety of settings. Nonetheless, it is not the best choice for large or long-lived plants, or those much better adapted to drier conditions.

Aeroponics

Comparable to the NFT, aeroponic systems have bare plant roots suspended in little or no growing medium. Instead of moving via the system, the nutrient solution is consistently misted on the put on hold origins, allowing for optimum uptake of water, nutrients, and oxygen. This is possibly the most efficient distribution system, however additionally one of the most costly. Like the drip system, numerous small parts need to be purchased, cleaned, and maintained. Nonetheless, if you can afford the first outlay, this system will most likely offer you the very best outcomes for your financial investment.

Beginning

If you're still not sure which of the many techniques of hydroponics are best suited to your strategies, start with a tiny, standard system and also end up being comfortable with hydroponic methods before you attempt to grow or invest way too much money in the current, most excellent system. Hydroponic gardening needs experience regulating nutrient degrees, water pH, light levels, moisture as well as even interior parasite control. Learning more about your plants and materials before you handle a mammoth task will reduce stress and anxiety, relieve the understanding curve as well as ensure a successful very first crop.

Interior Horticulture Techniques

A little plant inside your house improves interior air top quality as well as can lift spirits. Any part of your home that gets direct or indirect sunlight for about four or more hours can accommodate plants adapted to such conditions. With the introduction of effective synthetic lights, soilless growing media, as well as automated watering systems, interior gardening has matured.

Container Horticulture With Soil

Big, free-standing containers or built-in planters can provide lots of room for a mini garden in which various plants can cohabit. Interior container horticulture is among one of the most preferred ways to grow plants inside. The container can be metal, plastic or ceramic, or fabricated from concrete, yet you need to duplicate every little thing else that Nature offers to follow up with this strategy.

Light - Locate the containers in a sunny spot, such as a south-facing home window or a sunroom. Building a lean-to greenhouse against a big window or entrance will undoubtedly make it a well-lit expansion to your indoor room.

Watering - Water individual plants with a long-spouted watering can. If you forget to water, you might wind up losing many plants at one go, not to mention the mess involved. Drip irrigation is the solution to this trouble.

Soil - A loose dirt framework enables excellent drainage as well as air blood circulation around the roots. Formulate the potting soil according to the particular demands of your plants. Herbaceous plants with great roots do well in high dirt, but cacti and succulents require a rough mix. Readymade potting mixes take the uncertainty from it.

Temperature level control - House plants generally thrive at 75 to 85 degrees. Although they can tolerate reduced temperatures, providing additional warmth can enhance efficiency, which makes a distinction with vegetables. The hot pad inside the containers can give extra warmth to the origin area of the plants.

Growing optimum plants in the smallest room are the catalyst behind vertical horticulture, which is likewise a type of container horticulture. Ornamentals or vegetable plants are planted in containers that can be stacked or hooked onto a frame. Indoor wall surfaces that get an excellent quantity of sunlight can be the background of vertical yards or grow lights that can be utilized. Upright yards are usually sprinkled by drip irrigation or a wicking system integrated into the design.

Aggregate Solutions

Accumulated systems use inert materials such as Rockwool, clay pebbles, crushed rock, and so on to sustain plant origins. The media used to support the plant and likewise enables good oxygen penetration to the sources along with preserving a thin movie of nutrients and water.

The flooding, as well as drain method, is one of the most commonly made use of the aggregate system. In this system, a container is full of accumulation and also plants, which are then flooded with a nutrient solution.

The service is after that drained pipes back into the nutrition reservoir by opening up a shutoff at the end of the container. The roots should be immersed for not more than 20 -30 minutes throughout each cycle.

One more widely made use of the aggregate system is the drip-feed approach. The vitamins and mineral remedy is continually pumped from a tank via a 1/2-inch watering tube. This tube branches into many 1/8-inch tubes that feed the service to containers that bring the accumulation and plants. The solution that might be in excess gets collected at the base of each box and is then returned to the nutrient reservoir.

TIPS ON USING HYDROPONIC TECHNIQUES

Horticulture is one area that has been in a consistent state of advancement, given that the start of time. Right from the primitive ages till today, the guy has tried to find up with much better methods to offer a much more efficient and also hassle-free gardening strategy. For many years the various additions have taken multiple forms and brand-new, and much better procedures arose. Hydroponics is one such approach.

Hydroponics allows you to grow your plants all year long with no all-natural hassles. Standard gardening techniques require a variety of uncontrollable external factors for developing plants. Unmanageable variables like numerous seasons, weather conditions, etc. all play a vital function in the yield. However, methods that utilize water remedy for growing plants as opposed to soil decreases the risk included in such aspects.

These Hydroponics systems can be made in the comfort of your very own home if you're a seasoned gardener experienced with plants. You can additionally go with the business made kits available online. These packages can be found in numerous sizes, and you can select according to your specific needs. These sets will have the crucial equipment and also things like lights, pumps, containers, nutrient systems and so on. Regardless, you will require a deep understanding of plants and the numerous facets associated with their development and also survival.

Various elements make the process of Hydroponics systems an effective one. Lighting is one such crucial and essential facet. You must offer ample light for the plants to grow. Young plants ought to access least an excellent 8 hours of sunlight for efficient development. Keep in mind that excess of anything misbehaves. Consequently, make sure that the amount of light is not excessive, particularly when making use of several fires.

Moisture and also temperature are various other very vital factors in Hydroponics. Every living microorganism has a perfect level of numerous atmosphere conditions like moisture, temperature level, etc. When growing plants indoors, you must keep an excellent setting for the plants to grow. You can also introduce more carbon dioxide to the plant for far better development. In addition to extreme conditions, nourishment is additionally just as vital. By researching extra on the plants you prepare to grow, you will undoubtedly be able to have a far better understanding of their nutritional requirements.

When you have the needed nutrient option in Hydroponics, you will certainly have to concentrate on the price of absorption. This is to guarantee whether the plant will be able to absorb the nutrients to the best of its capability with no hassles. The entire point of having a controlled setting is to have the power to alter every single variable regarding growing plants to optimize its performance. Air pumps, as well as tubes, can assist in developing much better air blood circulation within the service.

Besides, the water made use of at the same time can likewise be re-utilized again and again. Although it is much better encouraged to have some sort of a horticulture experience before utilizing the Hydroponics, novices can also go with this procedure in a smaller sized magnitude to grow their preferred plants and vegetables.

HOW TO CHOOSE THE BEST
SUITABLE FOR YOUR BUDGET

If you have an interest in hydroponic horticulture, you will require to utilize the very best tools to have any kind of possibility of success. Relying on your degree of experience, offered spending plan, and also gardening demands, you can choose among the many different types of hydroponic systems available. Nonetheless, as you will observe, several of the crucial little bits of tools made use of to construct different systems are similar.

Picking the very best of essential hydroponics tools, as figured out by your particular gardening needs, will help make the work of standing out at hydroponics much easier. Below's a break down of essential hydroponics tools made use of in the majority of systems, accompanied by some useful pointers on just how to select the most effective of each.

The Tank

The reservoir used in hydroponic systems holds the water that consequently contains the nutrients to be supplied to your plants. As the most standard element of any type of hydroponic system, the reservoir retains the water that is required to keep your plants awash with wetness and minerals.

Depending upon your budget, in addition to the size of your operation, the storage tank can be anything from an expensive commercial variation or a straightforward container. To avoid dissipation of the water held therein, which would undoubtedly impact the vitamins and mineral balance, make sure to select a storage tank that features a lid. Additionally, the best reservoir needs not to be metal as it may lead to the introduction of unsafe minerals into the nutrient service, or the event of chemical reactions that might end up hurting your plants.

Water Pump

To supply your plants with the water and minerals they require to endure; you need to get your hands on a dependable water pump. Both primary kinds of water pumps are submersible and also non-submersible. The former is mounted in the nutrient option while the latter needs to be installed outside the service.

Water pumps are likewise classified according to their outcome in Gallons Per Min (GPM) or Gallons Per Hour (GPH). If you have a little established, after that, a pump that delivers around 30 to 40 GPH will be able to provide your plants with the water they need, as well as won't cost a lot.

Make sure to likewise think about the price at which water drains from the grow media when choosing a water pump that satisfies the wanted level of result.

Timer

In the majority of hydroponic systems, except one of the most fundamental ones, a timer is called for to help with the regulation of several essential features. For example, a timer can be made use of to manage to water, ventilation as well as illumination cycles.

When selecting the very best timer for your system, you will undoubtedly have two main choices, more accessible, and also a lot more inexpensive analog systems or more expensive, more advanced digital devices. The later is best for those aiming to create a system for growing fragile plants that require the utmost accuracy throughout the execution of each operation.

Lights

To increase plant growth, you need to have the best grow lights. It is essential to point out at this point that although fluorescent lights can be utilized to supplement all-natural light, they can not, on their own, give the spectrum of light needed by plants. Metal Halide, as well as High-Pressure Sodium Lights, were developed to produce a range of light that imitates the top quality of fire rising from the sun. Steel Halide lights are the closest you can get to sunshine. They produce even more a higher proportion of blue light that is fantastic for sustaining vegetative development.

High-pressure sodium lights, on the other hand, generate light that covers more of the red-orange spectrum. They last longer, shed brighter, and eat a reduced amount of energy than their steel halide counterparts, even though they create a narrower range of light.

For the results, it is recommended that you combine the use of both sorts of lights to provide the light that is as close as possible to the full spectrum of sunshine. Also, you can utilize light reflectors and moving companies to cover a more extensive room with fewer lights.

Growth Media

Dirt has no place in hydroponics; inert, non-organic products are utilized in its place. The growth media is made use of to sustain the plant as it grows. The medium chosen must, along with anchoring the plants, assist in the appropriate drain and also aeration of the origins. Polyurethane foam, perlite, bark, gravel, vermiculite, and even coconut fiber are several of your main options below.

The appropriate growth tool ought to be thick enough to secure the plant, yet not a lot that it prevents the blood circulation of air as well as the nutrient service. The fragments of the medium must have the ability to hold dampness and nutrients enough time to permit the roots to absorb the essential level of nutrients between flooding. Lastly, it must be clean and sterile to prevent the breeding of conditions, parasites, and also parasites.

128

pH Examination Kit

You require to keep the pH balance of the nutrient solutions to have any possibility of growing a healthy and balanced hydroponic garden. Even though some plants might have the ability to thrive at a lower or higher pH degree, it is advised that you keep it at between 6 and also 6.5. This indicates that you need to get a pH examination kit. Of all the hydroponic equipment discussed above, these sets are the most budget-friendly, but likewise among the most vital.

Growing a hydroponic yard includes less work than building a yard in the dirt. Nevertheless, to prosper, you need to have the best hydroponics equipment from the start, regardless of whether you pick to choose a prefabricated kit or are planning on putting together your own system little by little.

How hydroponic gardening works

Before you get going with your hydroponics yard, you require to comprehend a few points. Otherwise, you risk investing a great deal of time and money, as well as not obtaining the return you 'd expected. Besides, there's even more to gardening than just getting the right hydroponics nutrients as well as a lot of various other materials. You need to locate the correct configuration for your situation. There's a great deal of potential in hydroponic horticulture, but it isn't necessarily easy. Look at some of the most typical troubles you can expect to run into with your hydroponics yard.

Expenditure - It can be very costly to set up your hydroponics yard. The devices simply to begin requires some substantial financial investment. The cost of the garden goes down over time, yes, but you need to understand what it costs likely to take to set things up. Do not get into this kind of gardening with the misunderstanding that it's cheap. While a hydroponic garden often creates much better than a soil garden, it's not much less expensive.

Maintenance - You'll require to carry out regular upkeep if you desire your yard to work correctly. Unlike dirt gardens, which do things by themselves, your hydroponics systems will undoubtedly break down without conventional treatment. How much time will you need for upkeep? It depends upon the sort of policy you purchase. A lot of will certainly need at the very least a little everyday focus, which can cause travel problems. It can be challenging to discover garden-sitter.

Illness - Hydroponics gardens do have a reduced chance of particular varieties of diseases, mainly if you practice mindful control. That does not mean they're devoid of infection, though. Nevertheless, all the plants share the very same nutrient remedy. If a waterborne illness gets in, it can spread very quickly via your hydroponics systems. While this isn't an issue for yards that are meticulously maintained free of pollutants, it can be a big concern if you allow yourself to get careless.

Expertise - You have to have more background understanding to grow a hydroponics garden effectively. Soil-based yards are less complex for newbies. It is a great deal of enjoyment to get this understanding, yet it does take some work. Bear in mind - you can't grow every plant by doing this, and you require to know a whole lot concerning what you can grow. Every plant has various lights, nutrients, and treatment demands.

Do these mistakes imply you can not have your hydroponics yard? Not if you take the time to learn what you need to recognize first. While you do require some fundamental sources, there are a lot of magnificent gardens around that can work for you. Whether you want a rotating Volksgarden kind system or a typical hydroponic yard, you can get things growing!

If you've ever before put a plant clipping into a glass of water in the hopes that it will undoubtedly create roots, you have exercised in a kind of hydroponics. It is a branch of agriculture in which plants are grown without using dirt. The nutrients that the plants typically derive from the soil are simply dissolved right into the water instead, and depending upon the sort of hydroponic system made use of, the plant's origins are put on hold in, flooded with or misted with the nutrient remedy to ensure that the plant can obtain the aspects it requires for development.'

The term hydroponics stems from the old Greek "hydros," indicating water, and "ponos," meaning job. It can, in some cases, be mistakenly referred to as tank farming or aquaculture. Still, these terms are much more appropriately made use of for other branches of science that have nothing to do with horticulture.

As the populace of our world soars and also cultivable land readily available for crop manufacturing declines, hydroponics will undoubtedly offer us a lifeline of kinds as well as enable us to create crops in greenhouses or multilevel structures devoted to farming. Currently, where the cost of land is at a price, plants are being produced underground, on rooftops, and in greenhouses utilizing hydroponic methods.'

Possibly you want to begin a garden to make sure that you can grow your very own veggies, yet you don't have space in your backyard, or you're bewildered by bugs as well as bugs. This article will certainly equip you with the expertise you need to successfully establish a hydroponics yard in your home and provide recommendations of plants that will undoubtedly grow conveniently without a significant investment.

The idea of hydroponic horticulture (gardening without soil), has been around since the moment of King Solomon. There are a couple of advantages with hydroponic horticulture over typical horticulture -for instance, the price of development of a hydroponic plant can be up to 50% faster than a soil plant grown under the very same problems.

And the production of the plant is also higher!

The factor for this is that the plants get their nourishment fed straight right into their roots from nutrient-rich water. Because this water is so high in vitamins and mineral web content, the plant does not require great sources to search for nutrition. And also, considering that the plant uses up much less energy in growing origins, it has more power available to be efficient over the roofline! Hydroponically grown vegetables are healthy, vigorous, and also consistently reliable. This type of gardening is clean and even extremely simple, and it needs minimal effort.

Hydroponic horticulture is additionally beneficial to the atmosphere. For example, hydroponic gardening makes use of substantially much less water than dirt horticulture as a result of the consistent reuse of the nutrient services. And additionally, fewer chemicals are needed in hydroponic plants -they are not as essential. And topsoil erosion is not also an issue given that hydroponic gardening systems use no topsoil.

How exactly does a hydroponically grown plant obtain its nourishment -nourishment it usually gets from the dirt? Well, these nutrients can be found in liquid or powdered mixes and can be purchased at a hydroponic supply store. As well as like soil, hydroponic systems can be fed with organic or chemical nutrients. But you should know that a natural hydroponic system can be substantially even more job to preserve given that the natural substances tend to clump.

Hydroponic systems are generally categorized as passive or energetic. An energetic hydroponic system relocates the nutrient option with a pump. A passive hydroponic system relies upon the capillary action of the growing tool or a wick.

In a passive system, the abundant nutrient option is taken in by the medium and passed along to the plant's roots. Yet a drawback with this approach is that they usually are also wet and do not provide enough oxygen to the origin system for the very best growth prices. Hydroponic systems are additionally identified as recuperation or non-recovery. In recovery systems, the nutrient service is re-circulated for reuse. In a non-recovery order, nonetheless, the nutrient solution is not recuperated.

You may be uncertain of whether to get or build a hydroponic system. If you have a 'design mind' and also wish to construct one, consider acquiring one first simply to obtain accustomed to the internal operations. Acquire a system that does not cost a great deal of money. It will offer you an understanding of exactly how hydroponics works, and the hands-on experience can be worth the cost of the system as you will have the ability to reuse the parts when you choose to construct one.

If you have simply gone into the gardening scene after that, you may have come across a unique process called hydroponic horticulture. This particular kind of horticulture assists plants grows in a water-based environment. In it, we will take a look at three valuable pointers one can follow to create an effective hydroponic gardening system.

The initial idea is to see to it you are entirely geared up with the knowledge of how hydroponic systems work. A lot of individuals fail because they just do not comprehend precisely how plants grow in a water-based atmosphere—for instance, one key factor for failing results from the inaccurate input of water. You must get the best equilibrium of nutrients as well as water. It is also essential to select the best plants. One needs to remember that a hydroponic horticulture system is not suitable for each sort of plant. Some plants grow faster than others when placed in a water atmosphere.

The 2nd idea of producing a successful hydroponic garden is to make sure that atmosphere variables are evaluated as ideal degrees. One means of doing this is by making use of specialized garden tents. These outdoor tents can aid with controlling variables such as temperature level, light intensity, as well as humidity. It is imperative to change the water often. If you keep using the very same water, then that can cause plant growth problems. It is also vital that you alter the nutrients a minimum of once each week. If you maintain using the same remedy over and over after that, they will no more be beneficial.

The last suggestion is to select the appropriate system. There are several hydroponic systems one can choose. As an example, novices can go with a wick system. This particular system is quite essential as it does not call for individual devices such as pumps and also aerators. One merely has to put the plant in a large pot and also make use of a unique mat to make sure that the nutrients are being soaked up by the roots. Various other systems you ought to additionally understand consist of deepwater society systems as well as leading drip systems. Leading drip systems are mostly reusing systems. Nutrients from a reservoir storage tank fall into the plant with a single tube. Once the nutrients have been taken in, the option returns to the reservoir storage tank. If you utilize these tips after that, you will undoubtedly have a terrific beginning to developing a useful water-based garden.

All of us love to have a garden of our very own with fruits & vegetables being grown. However, it may not be feasible for individuals who stay in areas where the climate gets much less sunshine & other external elements that may decrease plant growth. Invite to interior hydroponics gardening, the best means to meet your desire to have your very own indoor garden with developing flowers.

The interior hydroponics gardening jobs round the

year throughout without worrying about frequent weather changes, no dirt is needed & that leads the plant to be chemical-free. So, one can grow herbs, fruits, vegetables as well as flowers as per their requirements.

Indoor hydroponics gardening has been so preferred that it not just taken just as a leisure activity; however, additionally a profession. To have an indoor Hydroponics yard, one may encounter great deals of questions or queries related to it like

- Which Fertilizer to be made use of?

- Which Yard grow lights are matched to your house?

- Where to acquire the hydroponics growing systems?

- How are the setup and maintenance done?

Allow us to share a few ideas on these locations, providing you a faint idea of where to start or exactly how to start an Interior hydroponics garden. A healthy indoor hydroponics gardening will certainly include mostly these elements - a pump to manage water, tank, a growing tray & a pump to provide the oxygen and also nutrients.

Most of us understand that hydroponics gardening does not require soil, yet to secure the plants or sustain the roots, we can utilize a soil-like tool such as fiber. See to it that the hydroponics system is porous, and after that, it can handle the appropriate retention of water as well as air. Next comes is the number of fertilizers or those high-quality nutrients that will certainly be needed for the nutrition of the plants & increasing its growth. One might understand which those nutrients are; they are only minerals like magnesium-calcium, iron, sulfur, zinc, copper, manganese, and also cobalt.

Then one ought to additionally take the factor to consider the pH balance of the plant, which is essential. There need not be any fluctuations in it, or else it may influence the plant, thus reducing its development price.

The nutrition service can be prepared in your home by bringing all the active ingredients offered in the marketplace. Of course, the mixing takes a while; therefore, the majority of them prefer to get the same from the market that is already mixed. One gets even more information about the nutrients, pH level as well as other sets associated with interior hydroponics gardening by searching on the Internet.

The next vital point that a person has to pay attention to indoor hydroponics horticulture is to make sure the correct light and air are available to the plants. One ought to also know the ideal spectrum of light that will be required for the interior gardening as well as based on that; the lights need to be bought from the marketplace.

One needs to not worry about the amount of water that might be required; there are automated controls offered that will only spray to the roots of the plants at regular intervals. This way, water does not clog & this prevents the decomposing of the sources. A checklist of benefits by doing Indoor Hydroponics Gardening is mentioned right here -

- Much less upkeep

- Chemical & disease-free

- Maximum yield or create

- High level of sustainability

- Taste much better

- Less space need

- Environmentally-friendly

- Minor water need

- Low carbon exhausts

- Balanced & consistent plant growth

- High nutritional value generate

The fruits and vegetables that are grown interior hydroponics gardening preference better than those grown in soil. One can also grow plants and vegetables at any time or any kind of period of the year. That is why this treatment has brought in lots of yard farmers who are interested in having their very own indoor hydroponics garden. Herbs & veggies like cucumbers, lettuce, tomatoes, and also peppers are all suitable for indoor horticulture.

All these need very little room, like even as smaller such as a windowsill. Long-term rewards are predicted if the procedure of indoor hydroponics horticulture is done correctly by discovering the keys and also getting the experience over an amount of time.

THE BEST PLANTS TO HAVE IN YOUR SETUP

I f you have ever before asked, " What can I grow with Hydroponics?" probably, the answer is you can grow anything. That holds true. However, not many will undoubtedly thrive in a water-based setting, while others will never reach their full capacity. Well, today I'm going to make it very easy for you to choose the best plants to begin.

1. Lettuces

Lettuces, the excellent active ingredient for the salad sandwich in your kitchen area, are probably the most typical veggies that are grown in Hydroponics. They grow very fast in a hydroponic system and also are rather simple to care for. Lettuces can be built in any Hydroponics system, consisting of the NFT, Aeroponics, Ebb & Flow, etc. This veggie is no question a great plant if you just begin with Hydroponics.

2. Tomatoes

Several types of plants, including typical and cherry ones, have been grown commonly by Hydroponic hobbyists and industrial farmers. Botanically, the plant is a fruit, yet most individuals, whether vendors or customers, consider it as vegetables. One thing is that tomatoes require more sunlight. So you should be prepared to purchase some grow lights if you intend to grow inside your home.

3. Radishes

Radishes are another vegetable that makes an excellent flavoring mix with various other plants. Radishes are just one of the most convenient plants to grow - either in dirt or hydroponics. It's far better to start from seeds, as well as you can see seedlings within 3 - 7 days. Radishes flourish in significant temperature levels as well as do not need any kind of lights.

4. Kale

Kale is an incredibly nourishing as well as a delicious-flavored plant for the house and also dining establishment dishes. It is a beautiful veggie for a healthy and balanced person with tested health and wellness benefits. The fantastic news is that people have growed Kale hydroponically for so many years, so absolutely, you can do it in the water supply. And in fact, it's simple to grow as well as flourish well in this system.

5. Cucumbers

Cucumbers are a typical vining plant that is grown in the house and the industrial greenhouses. They take pleasure in a fast development under sufficient condition and also hence give very high returns. There are several kinds and sizes of cucumbers, consisting of the insensitive American slicers, long thin-skinned seedless European, as well as the smooth-skinned Lebanese cucumbers. All can grow well in Hydroponics. Cucumber is a cozy plant, so be sure to supply it with enough light and also a temperature level.

6. Spinaches

The favored veggie that can be either eaten raw or prepared in your meal does grow well in the water-based environment. Spinach is an exotic plant, so it does not need way too much light. You can gather everything at the same time or detach some leaves. You can have 12 weeks of constant harvesting under a good condition of climate as well as a growing setting.

7. Beans

One of the most low-maintenance vegetables that can be grown hydroponically. You can choose the kinds of seeds you can grow, including environment-friendly beans, pole beans, pinto beans, lima beans. You will undoubtedly require a trellis or something to sustain the plants if you plant pole beans. Seed germination takes typically 3 - 8 days. Harvesting begins after 6 - 8 weeks. After that, you can continue the plant for 3 - 4 months.

8. Chives

It's simpler to grow chives from a plant in a Hydroponic system. So better to get them from your regional yard supplies. Under a normal growing condition, it takes six to 8 weeks before it is completely mature. Then you can cultivate or harvest it regularly - it requires 3 - 4 weeks later to grow back completely. Chive calls for great deals of light, 12 - 14 hours of sun each day.

9. Basil

Basil prospers very well in a hydroponic system, and it is without a doubt among one of the most produced herbs in Hydroponic. You can grow basil in Drip system. As soon as this plant reaches the mature phase, you harvest and also cut it once a week. Basil needs lots of lights. It will undoubtedly go through a lousy development when you do not provide it with over 11 hrs of lightning.

10. Mints

Mints, mainly peppermint and also spearmint, have been growed extensively, whether in soils and even hydroponics. Their aromatic substances in mints are revitalizing, and poignant, which confirms their use as a flavor for food and drinks. Mint roots spread out so swiftly, making it excellent to grow with Hydroponics.

11. Strawberries

Strawberries are well fit for hydroponic growing. These fruits are one of the most popular plants growed in commercial hydroponic production. They have been grown in large NFT systems by the modern ranches for decades. Nevertheless, you can still enjoy delicious fresh strawberries to feed all your family members by increasing them in the house and collecting the fruits all year long.

12. Blueberries

Blueberries, a terrific fruit high in vitamins for your meal, can be growed well in Hydroponics. This plant takes longer to thrive than strawberries, commonly up until the second year.

13. Peppers

Peppers need the very same hydroponic growing condition like tomatoes - cozy temperature level as well as vast quantities of lights. Peppers usually take a couple of months to grow. You can either start growing them from seeds or plants from the local yard provider. Advised varieties for hydroponically developing are Jalapeno, Habanero for hot peppers, Mazurka, Cubico, Nairobi, Fellini for beautiful peppers.

Harder to grow

Again this does not indicate that you can not grow these kinds of plants; they are simply extra tough to grow in Hydroponics. Yet seasoned cultivators have built them in their soilless systems for many years and also appreciated outstanding yields.

Plants that occupy huge rooms.

If space is limited, it's ideal for preventing squash, melons, pumpkins, corn, and other big plants. It does not suggest that you can not grow these plants, but in a narrow area, it's more challenging to look after plants, and also, the yields are not as good as other locations where these plants have areas to grow.

Deep Root veggies

Again, it's hard to look after plants that need a great deal of depth for origin. So this is not suggested for newbies.

Potatoes, carrots, turnips come under these types.

For root crops, you need a substratum with adequate length as well as high deepness to sustain the origins, as well as these types of plants, have a tendency not to offer as good outcomes as they remain in the dirt. If you have a big growing environment like a greenhouse, patio area, you can establish an advanced system as well as grow big plants, root veggies, and many other hard-to-grow ones. That atmosphere is perfect for you to try with any type of plant.

Finishing up

As a person brand-new to Hydroponics, it would be smart to go with simple to grow plants that take pleasure in rapid development. We have discussed numerous examples over. As a consequence, you can obtain the outcome and learn the experience quick, after that feel influenced to relocate to something harder.

Experienced Hydroponic garden enthusiasts might have a proper understanding of the Hydroponics systems as well as the plants' kind they are going to grow. They can strive for other plants like cigarette, massive melons, pumpkins, sunflowers, and more. There are no restrictions. A yard calls for client labor and also interest. Plants do not grow simply to satisfy aspirations or to accomplish excellent intentions. They flourish because somebody expended initiative on them.

Freedom Hyde Bailey

Selecting a plant to grow in your Hydroponic garden is simply the primary step. You will require proper expertise to establish the system. And also most significantly, the plants depend upon you for their survival. That needs substantial common interest and also persistence until you get the returns, similar to anything beneficial in life. If you wish to sum up the primary hydroponic plants you can start, I have made an in-depth infographic concerning plants (vegetables, fruits, natural herbs) that are best matched in Hydroponics.

HOW TO MAINTAIN YOUR
HYDROPONIC SYSTEM

Keeping the correct pH in the stream of your hydroponic system protects against an adverse chemical reaction to plant foods within the watering lines. A high pH level can often obstruct within the lines and cause significant issues for your hydroponic system. pH represents "prospective hydrogen," suggesting the concentration of favorably billed hydrogen ions relative to adversely charged hydroxyl ions in a compound. Hydrogen ions are naturally acidic, while hydroxyl ions are fundamental; maintain these truths in mind both as you construct your hydroponic as well as during your grow process.

The pH range goes from 0-14 a score 7 in this array means that the pH level is neutral. Anything below 7 suggests an acidic compound, as well as anything about 7, which shows an alkaline compound. Your hydroponic needs to have a neutral status or a rating of 7 as usual as possible. Examples of acids consist of nitric acid or phosphoric acid, which, when included in water, have a "fierce" response in which the compound disintegrates or ionizes. When referring to the strength of the acid, this remains regarding ionization they experience.

In North America, most water supplies are alkaline in nature; this is an advantage considering that several plants favor a more fundamental setting near their origin structure. If a plant absorbs nitrate ions that are adversely charged, the origins will undoubtedly drop the negatively billed hydroxyl ions to establish electrical equilibrium. This will increase the pH level of the surrounding origin atmosphere. If positively charged ammonium ions are absorbed undoubtedly, billed ions will be dropped, creating a rise in the acidity of the origin environment. Knowing how your plant cleanses itself when it comes to its acidic atmosphere is vital when running your hydroponic system.

As you consider your pH improvement methods bear in mind that the pH level of the water is not the only variable to consider. The buffering capability of your plant or its capacity to stand up to pH modifications requires to be observed ultimately when setting up your hydroponic system. Remember that typically numerous plant food components are acidic in nature as well as others are alkaline. When attempting to attain the proper pH balance with fertilizer alone, make sure to make use of water with as little bicarbonate as feasible. An additional point to bear in mind while maintaining your hydroponic system is that when phosphorous levels climb, they can cause the presence of magnesium and calcium within your water.

There are various methods to check for pH levels in your hydroponic systems, amongst one of the most economical as well as most comfortable ways to inspect you pH level are "pH strips," they are reactive strips that you soak in your water to reveal the present pH degree. The piece will have a chemical reaction with the water and also display where your hydroponic system's pH level is on a scale of 0-14. Do not take too lightly the importance of keeping correct pH equilibrium within your hydroponic system; it is crucial to the growth price as well as total health and wellness of your plants.

Evaluating the nutrition balance of your liquid solution must be done at the very least every three days. There are several methods to examine the pH of the nutrient service in your hydroponic system. Paper test strips are possibly one of the most low-cost ways to inspect the pH of the nutrient solution. Liquid pH examination kits are one of the most prominent approaches for the pastime garden enthusiast. One of the most sophisticated ways to examine pH is to make use of the digital meters. One of the most popular kinds of the meter is the electronic pen. Checking the level of water in your system container ought to be done at least every three days. When including water to the system, first improve that water with your nutrient option, or you will thin down the container fluid as well as throw the proper nutrient balance into a tail-spin.

You ought to daily examine the plants for growth patterns and to see if any type of parasites or disease has actually attacked your plants ... and afterward quickly do whatever is needed to neutralize the infection or deficiency.

When plants are fully growed (particularly natural herbs), you must consider covering or clipping the plants at the ideal time to make sure that the plant will certainly acquire brand-new vigor, grow even better, and also you will undoubtedly get the trimmings for use in your cooking. Naturally, harvest any kind of ripe or developed natural herbs, fruits, or veggies so that the plant will grow more generate. Also, you will, after that, have the advantage of vine-ripened enhancements to your kitchen.

Be ever aware of the intensity of light, whether sunlight or human-made light and wind where the plants are growing so that you can change for excesses of those things, such as including or removing screen cloth, or relocating the system to a new secured area, as they could harm the plants. Likewise, if the plants have been subjected to rain, check your nutrient levels quickly to stay clear of dilution of your liquid sources.

Attempt to check your unit at the time the pumping system ought to begin always to ensure the pump is working as well as efficient to supply the nutrients to your plants. Alter the nutrition storage tank a minimum of every three weeks.

Periodically, flush a mix of tidy water as well as hydrogen peroxide via your system to maintain the piping clean and also free of damaging buildup. You need to keep the cleanliness of your system whatsoever times.

Just how to grow hydro is correct regarding how to preserve your nutrient tank. You can only offer all the most effective conditions, relax, and allow plant growth to take place. Assume your plants are obtaining sufficient light and air, as well as are maintained a high temperature. Plant growth will happen (often promptly) as long as you supply the best problems in your nutrient service (and also in the remainder of the grow room) daily!

Via the water, the plants will obtain every one of their food. This water needs to contain primary nutrients, additional nutrients (Calcium, Magnesium, Iron, Sulfur), and all trace nutrients. I strongly suggest using a specialist hydroponic nutrient item for this.

In addition to primary food, there are a few additives that make a big difference in the healthy growth of your plants. These are vitamins trace nutrient supplements, and also plant hormonal agents (in both seaweed as well as Prosper Active red). An additional useful additive is Silica, which is made use of to increase the immune system of plants. Vitamin B1 is not a nutrient salt, yet it drives cellular division (plant development). Use it in every decline of water from start to finish!

Several professional gardening write-ups I have checked out by individuals who recognize how to grow hydro suggest including Thrive Alive B1 and also Maxicrop to every decrease of water you provide your plants. Use 10 ml per gallon of each. If you are using a seaweed-based plant food, it is not necessary to include extra fluid seaweed. For more details on feeding and also keeping your nutrient solution, check out the hydroponic nutrients web page.

Let's start by answering the concern of what hydroponics is? Well, hydroponics is a progressed means of cultivating plants using a remedy full of nutrients; with this brand-new method of growing, the use of dust or dirt is omitted.

If you enjoy to garden but face numerous troubles such as minimal space, bugs, or unsuitable weather conditions after that, hydroponics is your response. Hydroponics permits you to grow your yard indoors with exceptionally high success prices.

Nowadays, hydroponics has become a pastime for lots of individuals, because of the simpleness of its function and the advantages it has when compared to the typical way of gardening. Here are numerous benefits of having a hydroponic yard:

You don't require to have great deals of area to grow your plants. Hydroponics takes up a little space and practically permits you to position it anywhere you see fit. There is no need for a lot of water, considering that there is no dirt for the water to be absorbed before it reaches the plant's roots. Hydroponics is ideal for locations with water restrictions. Using hydroponics saves water; when you water a healthy garden, just 10% of the water you utilize will undoubtedly end up at your plant's origins.

You will spend as minimum time as feasible maintaining your hydroponics garden. Once you have established your hydroponics garden, you will certainly require to invest a little time on the nutrient option. You no longer need to be strained by parasites and finding an appropriate service or plant diseases such as fungi. Your hydroponics garden can be kept inside your home away from all these godawful problems.

Plant Species That Can Grow in Hydroponics. There are numerous amounts of plants that you can grow in a hydroponics yard. You can grow herbs, veggies such as lettuce, tomatoes, cucumbers, peppers; you can improve your favorite flowers and even fruit. Hydroponics can grow a massive bulk of plants; however, do keep in mind that plants that climb up must be provided added assistance.

The benefits of organic farming

When you think about going eco-friendly and also going natural when it pertains to the food that you consume day-to-day, possibly you will certainly state it is challenging, or is there something as organic nowadays. This are just several of the acquainted lines which you will learn through people that do not know natural farming. Chemical-free farming is simply specified as going back in time where people ranch and make use of natural material for their farm, manure as well as garden compost, to name a few. The benefits of natural farming are apparent, which is why a lot of farmers are currently into organic crop production. Its advantages do not only cover humans but the atmosphere also.

Plants and pet which have actually been planted and also elevated the all-natural method, have much more nutrients and mineral contrasted to industrialized ones. These farm items can keep you healthy and balanced, as well as will certainly allow you to avoid illness. The prices of these products are also competitive, which is why a lot of customers buy these due to the cost as well as the health and wellness advantages it gives. When you opt to purchase usually grown products, you can be sure that it is devoid of chemical deposit, hazardous compounds and also ingredients which are confirmed dangerous and also can create health problems like specific kind of cancer cells.

Organic farming, not just profit customers yet also the environment, when you use manure and even compost in making your plants healthy and balanced, you aid the soil to prosper with nutrients. It can also advantage livestock, poultry, and also dairies since when animal feed on naturally growed yards, they grow healthier as well as generate more and even healthier meat as well as eggs. The products from chemical-free farming are of far better taste too.

Organic farming is lower in expense because you will not utilize any type of pricey chemicals in this procedure. You will undoubtedly make the most of what nature has given us. In conventional farming, weeds are gotten rid of the use of pesticides. The longer you will certainly utilize these chemicals, the higher the probability that the unwanted lawn will be immune to that chemical and will go on returning. You have to use a more powerful kind of chemical, which will undoubtedly include damages to the environment.

The many benefits of returning to the basic style of farming must not be disregarded and also need to be practiced once again, for us to be much healthier as well as live longer and also for the atmosphere to be restored from all the damages which are caused by automation and even traditional farming.

If you wish to have much healthier poultry products, use natural chicken feed. Organic hog feed will provide you top quality of pork meat without investing way too much; you can buy this online today.

Organic farming is a fantastic endeavor for anybody that wishes to grow gorgeous and yummy veggies by themselves land in an environmentally friendly method. The approaches for chemical-free agriculture incorporate the knowledge of ecology and contemporary farming modern technology with typical farming techniques based upon usually happening organic processes. This kind of agriculture makes use of several methods to improve the fertility of the dirt. These approaches consist of crop turning, cover cropping, as well as the application of nutrient-rich compost. Unlike popular beliefs, natural farming can compete with standard farming methods fairly successfully in growing corn, soybeans, wheat, barley as well as various other grains along with many types of vegetables and fruits.

Organic plant foods are an integral part of a chemical-free farming operation because the fertility of the dirt is essential to healthy and also plentiful crops. Organic fertilizers are made from many different kinds of naturally occurring substances such as bat guano, plume dish, as well as fish meal. Commercially made natural fertilizers consist of garden compost, blood meal, bone meal, humic acid, amino acids, brassin, and seaweed essences. The advantages of using organic plant foods are many. Yet, one of the significant benefits is that these fertilizers, as well as soils, are verified to be much better for your health and wellness as well as the setting and also will not influence the size of your yield. Organic fertilizers additionally have the advantage of not having particular troubles related to the heavy routine use of human-made plant foods. Reapplying human-made fertilizers regularly as well as with ever before boosting amounts to maintain dirt fertility becomes essential when synthetic plant foods are utilized. Also, eutrophication can occur, causing contaminated water supplies as well as big scale fish kills. Because of their all-natural makeup, natural fertilizers enhance physical as well as biological nutrients in dirt and assist the earth to retain them, thus lessening the threats of over-fertilization.

Organic farming might be most widely identified as what methods it does not make use of like synthetic fertilizers and also artificial herbicides; however, it is more crucial to specify chemical-free farming by the approaches that are being made use of. Farming naturally requires the advancement and preservation of an environmental system where issues are resolved naturally. Also, this balance is kept through the correct execution and monitoring of such methods. It has become the fastest growing sectors of the farming industry in the United States just recently as well as today, the vision of organic agriculture as ecologically lasting farming exercised by tiny farmers is headed towards much more big range farming operations to supply ethically audio and also healthy and balanced food for several.

My name is William Moriarty, and I stay in the sunny south. South Carolina to be a lot more precise as well as I have a stunning story of land there that I am turning into an organic vegetable farm. I have created a blog on chemical-free farming as well as modern-day homesteading that I intend to construct for the direct future to make sure that I can document our progress and so that I might communicate with other like-minded individuals. I plan to learn all I can around this great lifestyle that I think will undoubtedly help us conquer several of the environmental issues that are impacting our globe today.

And today's industrialized agriculture, every little thing is concentrated on an optimum of temporary monetary revenue, no matter the eco-friendly as well as social repercussions. The use of herbicides, pesticides as well as chemical fertilizers ruins the health of the dirt and the wellness of individuals furthermore, leaving behind a farming dessert. Large international businesses, setting up substantial mono societies, cause severe damage to existing social structures as well as are accountable for the termination of countless types at an increasingly more accelerating speed.

The idea of natural farming, however, complies with a roadway right in various directions. At our organic ranch, the honesty of nature is taken into consideration the greatest treasure by both moral and economic criteria. The integrity of the environment surrounding us is an essential part of healthy and balanced living. People benefit not solely from fresh air, clean water, and also healthy food, yet too from the beauty of the landscape, an exceptionally essential advantage for the heart and even therefore for our physical wellness.

Consequently, natural farming intends firmly on the defense of nature. We are aware of economic necessities, yet we are significantly persuaded that regard for our natural deposits over time will certainly additionally prove to be a financial benefit. One of our crucial objectives currently is to maintain old olive trees, even if they are not any longer efficient, as well as to keep usually growed settings.

During the last decades, several of the old deserted olive groves around have been overgrown by Mediterranean macchia, a typical low woodland with the broom, wild roses, laurel, holm oaks as well as lots of various other trees and bushes. Therefore nature has formed a wide range of beautiful new mini settings. The clearing of this Mediterranean macchia, to reclaim the maximum manufacturing of olive oil, would create unjustified environmental damage.

In consequence, rather than concentrating on optimizing temporary financial earnings, it is our purpose to save the existing small environments with their unusual pets as well as plants. We make the olive trees meticulously accessible again and also provide the care they need for enduring and thriving without ruining the existing biodiversity. We are encouraged that this is an actual investment in our future and the future of our kids.

Dr. Annette Greifenhagen is a physician. Apart from her job as a therapist, she runs the organic farm as well as agriturismo Suite La Rogaia in Umbria, Italy. Vacation Home La Rogaia is an agriturismo positioned near Lago Trasimeno in Umbria, Italy. It provides vacation apartments or condos and also a variety of innovative classes, such as painting, dancing, genuine Italian cooking, Italian language training courses, and too numerous others. It uses additionally unique vacation occasions, like taking part in the olive harvest. Villa La Rogaia is likewise an organic farm that grows olive trees, creates the most excellent extra-virgin olive oil. You can take on an olive tree at La Rogaia.

Sustainability over the long term. Several adjustments observed in the atmosphere are long term, happening slowly with time. Organic agriculture considers the tool- and long-term result of farming treatments on the agro-ecosystem. It aims to produce food while making an eco-friendly balance to prevent soil fertility or pest troubles.

Organic agriculture takes a positive technique in contrast to treating issues after they arise.

Dirt structure methods such as crop rotations, inter-cropping, symbiotic associations, cover crops, natural plant foods, as well as minimum farming, are central to organic practices. These motivate soil fauna as well as vegetation, enhancing soil development as well as framework as well as creating even more stable systems. Subsequently, nutrient and also power biking is improved, and the absorbent abilities of the soil for nutrients and water are increased, compensating for the non-use of mineral plant foods. Such management strategies likewise play a vital function in controlling soil erosion.

The time that the soil is exposed to abrasive pressures is decreased, dirt biodiversity is raised, and also nutrient losses are lowered, aiding to keep and improve dirt efficiency. Plant export of nutrients is customarily made up of farm-derived renewable resources. Yet, it is sometimes needed to supplement natural soils with potassium, phosphate, calcium, magnesium, and also trace elements from outside sources.

In lots of farming areas, pollution of groundwater training courses with artificial plant foods and chemicals is a significant issue. As the use of these is forbidden in organic agriculture, they are replaced by natural plant foods (e.g., compost, pet manure, green manure) and also via the use of better biodiversity (in terms of species cultivated and even long-term greenery), enhancing dirt framework as well as water seepage. Well taken care of organic systems with far better nutrient absorbent capacities, substantially reduce the danger of groundwater contamination. In some locations where pollution is a genuine issue, conversion to natural agriculture is exceptionally motivated as a corrective measure (e.g., by the Federal governments of France and Germany).

Air and also environment modification. Organic agriculture minimizes non-renewable energy usage by decreasing agrochemical requirements (these call for high quantities of fossil fuel to be produced). Organic farming contributes to mitigating the greenhouse effect and also international warming via its ability to sequester carbon in the soil.

Numerous administration methods utilized by organic agriculture (e.g., minimal tillage, returning plant deposits to the dirt, the use of cover plants and also turnings, and even the higher combination of nitrogen-fixing beans), boost the return of carbon to the soil, elevating productivity as well as favoring carbon storage. A variety of studies disclosed that dirt organic carbon components under chemical-free farming are significantly higher.

The more organic carbon is preserved in the dirt, the much more the reduction capacity of agriculture versus environment adjustment is higher. Nevertheless, there is much research study needed in this field, yet. There is an absence of information on dirt natural carbon for developing nations, with no ranch system contrast information from Africa and also Latin America, and just minimal information on dirt natural carbon stocks, which is critical for figuring out carbon sequestration prices for farming practices.

Biodiversity. Organic farmers are both custodians and also users of biodiversity at all degrees. At the gene level, seeds and also types are chosen for their better resistance to conditions and also their durability to weather stress and anxiety.

At the types level, diverse combinations of plants and pets enhance nutrient and also energy biking for agricultural manufacturing. At the ecosystem degree, the maintenance of all-natural locations within and around organic areas, as well as the absence of chemical inputs, create appropriate habitats for wild animals. The constant use of under-utilized varieties (commonly as rotation plants to develop soil fertility) reduces the disintegration of agro-biodiversity, promoting a healthier genetics pool - the basis for future adaptation.

The arrangement of frameworks providing food as well as shelter, and also the absence of pesticide usage, attract new or re-colonizing types to the organic location (both long-term and also migratory), consisting of wild vegetations as well as animals (e.g., birds) as well as organisms beneficial to the natural system such as pollinators and insect killers. The number of studies on chemical-free farming and biodiversity increased substantially within the last years. A Recent Research Reporting On A Meta-Analysis Of 766 Scientific Documents wrapped up that chemical-free farming generates more biodiversity than other farming systems.

Genetically modified microorganisms. Making use of GMOs within organic systems is not permitted during any type of phase of health food production, processing, or handling. As the possible impact of GMOs on both the environment and also health and wellness is not understood, natural agriculture is taking the preventive technique and also selecting to urge natural biodiversity.

The original label, as a result, offers an assurance that GMOs have not been used purposefully in the manufacturing as well as handling of the organic items. This is something that can not be guaranteed in standard items as labeling the presence of GMOs in food products has not yet entered force in the majority of countries.

Nonetheless, with increasing GMO make use of in traditional farming and because of the technique of GMO transmission in the environment (e.g., via plant pollen), natural agriculture will not have the ability to make sure that essential items are GMO cost-free in the future. A comprehensive discussion on GMOs can be located in the FAO magazine "Genetically Changed Organisms, Customers, Food Security And Also The Setting."

Ecological solutions. The influence of natural farming on natural resources favors interactions within the agro-ecosystem that are vital for both agricultural production and nature preservation. Environmental solutions obtained include dirt creating as well as conditioning, soil stabilization, waste recycling, carbon sequestration, nutrients biking, predation, pollination, and habitats. By going with organic products, the consumer via his/her purchasing power advertises a much less contaminating agricultural system. The hidden costs of farming to the setting in terms of natural resource destruction are reduced.

HOW TO MANAGE THE CLIMATE, NUTRIENTS FOR YOUR CROPS

T here is a lot of hype regarding seed in the searching world today. Affixed to this buzz is a great deal of hunting stars declaring to utilize the "finest" or "most powerful" seed available. Sadly, they appear to transform their sponsors as well as kinds of seed higher than many folks change their undergarments.

Recent research studies have revealed that deer choose to eat plants from fields that are well dealt with. This consists of proper changing of soil as well as weed control.

No matter what speed you have chosen to use, how much cash you have spent on seed, or that's telling you they have a superior product, your efforts will always disappoint their prospective unless you have a strong foundation. I think if we have a higher understanding of the soil, we position our seed right into, the deficiencies

175

in the dirt, as well as just how to modify the earth appropriately, we will begin to satisfy as well as even surpass the goals we established as food-plotters, along with cutting total expenses.

We will start to see visible growth in plant return, have much better sampling plants with more all-natural sugars as well as healthy proteins, see even more water and nutrient retention in the dirt, as well as controlling the soil PH. This will undoubtedly lead to better moving of vitamins, minerals, as well as other required nutrition to the animals consuming our food plots.

Two of the main ingredients that comprise our soil are weathered rock and decaying microorganisms; both play a substantial part in its make-up and feature. Rocks are weathered both literally and chemically. Blowing sand, water, temperature level, as well as stress are all a part of the physical weathering process, where the rocks are broken down with no molecular adjustment in the minerals. Chemical weathering, however, does change the molecular composition of the metals. The primary opponent to minerals in the soil is a procedure referred to as hydrolysis, which is a chemical reaction in which a substance responds with water to produce various other materials.

Rainfall soaks up the carbon dioxide airborne as it drops, resulting in the production of a weak carbonic acid that is then moved from the rain to the mineral loaded soil. In the past, acids only were available in contact with the ground from the respiration of CARBON DIOXIDE from living organisms. Probably old sculptures give a more precise understanding of the effects of hydrolysis. These sculptures did disappoint very much deterioration until contemporary sectors started producing vast quantities of smoke, resulting in sulfuric and nitric acid in rainfall. Hydrolysis is the factor minerals are so depleted from the soil in lots of parts of the USA.

Whatever crops you plant, they are just moving agents. If the dirt does not contain the correct minerals and the capability to create proteins, the pets will never see the complete results of your planting. It prize whitetail growth is what you desire. Also, you do not intend to make use of available products to supply minerals to pets and repair depleted dirt; the process will undoubtedly be a lot longer. If the proper elements are not offered in the soil, the pet will not obtain them with the plants it is eating, leading to points like antler limitations, as well as age framework being closer to the top of your administration strategy. That is if they aren't already up there.

There are five consider soil development that is important in making top quality food plot decisions. The very first of these factors is parent products. What significant rock (sedimentary rock, sand, granite, and so on.) eroded to develop your dirt? These are essential details in figuring out what your earth already has, as well as what they do not have. Take sand, for instance. The ground on our farm is made mainly of sand, which indicates we will experience much more leeching than others. Because of this, we need to attempt and stay away from stories on grades that will undoubtedly raise leeching. We must also deal with recovering the natural products in the dirt profile; this will be a remarkable assistance in water as well as nutrient retention.

The 2nd aspect is the climate. Rain, as well as temperature level, are factors that not only help in dirt development, yet can likewise either aid you in your planting or battle against your efforts. For example, Extreme amounts of rainfall on a farm with sandy dirt equals more plant food required later in the year. Also, selecting plants with deep taproots like alfalfa or chicory would undoubtedly be a must.

The 3rd aspect is the living microorganisms in and around the soil. All organisms, plants, and also pets, large as well as small, are a significant component in soil formation and conservation. They influence soil fertility and both water as well as nutrient retention, in addition to regulation the soil's PH. This is usually a highly ignored subject in food story programs.

The topography is the 4th factor in dirt development. Soil is an all-natural function of your landscape. Your landscape determines how rapidly your grounds were developed, as well as what materials are in them. Recognizing this will undoubtedly assist you in choosing a terrific food plot place. Take the ever before high creek bottom as an example. Debris carried from water, in addition to more plant life rotting in the dirt, results in nutrients. The creek base goes to the receiving end of sandy soil as well as hill runoffs, creating a place with more plentiful and lush plant development.

The 5th, as well as the final factor in dirt formation, is time. Exactly how old is your dirt? Over here in the northeast, we have some of the most past range of mountains and soils in the USA. The longer the ground has been around, the longer the other elements have been affecting dirt formation. More youthful geological areas have the most abundant, weather condition able products that hold and gradually release nutrients to plant life; older locations will undoubtedly be much more diminished and should be amended.

We need to take a closer take a look at our soil horizon (soil layers) as well as see what we are managing, and also, along with our dirt examinations, use this knowledge to control dust to create much better and even much longer. I hope to help us to recognize that our foundation is not the seed or the construct from our tractor, but the very dust we stand and also work with. As we get this understanding and also placed it into the method, we will see high-quality results from our food plots that we would certainly not have seen otherwise. This, in turn, appears in body weight, antler growth, as well as total health of deer.

Think about it as placing your food plots on a well-designed wellness program. The highlight of climate adjustment in most countries worldwide is the increasing regularity of severe weather occasions such as unpredictable floodings, droughts, and other abiotic anxiety for crops. It is not surprising that many nations want technologies for adjusting agriculture to climate modification, and Ukraine is no exception.

However, traditional steps that exist worldwide method do not sufficiently think about the relevance of interactions between soil and also plants. As an example, from 138 projects of the European Environment Adaption System, just 16 are correlated with the dirt, but only one of them checks out the interaction in the "soil-plant" system. In this link, the primary purpose of our study was to establish the effectiveness of agrochemical techniques in plant nutrition management for plants adaptation to severe weather changes. The influence of different agrochemical procedures in the "soil-plant" system on the resilience of plants to various climate conditions of the growing period was examined in a lasting area experiment that was started in 1969.

The experiment was on a Chernozem at the Grakivske Speculative Station in the Kharkiv region, Ukraine. Soil samples were taken throughout the growing period from the field under different crops. Soil, as well as plant samples evaluations, included macro- as well as micronutrients web content, dirt wetness. Study in the field experiment has demonstrated a close relationship between the typical annual rains and material of readily available kinds of macronutrients in the dirt (particularly for nitrate-nitrogen the connection coefficient was 0.98) Studies have revealed that enhancing the yearly rainfall by 100 mm raises the web content of nitrate-nitrogen in the soil at 7 mg per kg. An additional relationship has shown that the declining amount of rain decreases the variety of the N:P and also; as a result, the schedule of these components to crops.

Hence, in drought conditions, the performance of the use of offered nutrients by crops depends upon the dirt dampness, and also water use effectiveness relies on the existence of the essential nutrients for the harvest. In our investigation, the adhering to agrochemical plant nourishment monitoring procedures were utilized. Creating a high phosphate level of the dirt contributes to the preservation of dirt wetness books by 4% more than in various other agricultural histories; optimizing making use of water by plants (using water per 1 lots of dehydrated matter is decreased by 20-25%); enhancing making use of nitrogen from the dirt to 18-30%. Application of integrated fertilizer system as an application macronutrient, trace elements, organic prep work, as well as humates in the essential stages of plant development, supplies a 60% yield boost in severe weather conditions.

The development of 2 strips of mineral plant foods application at different deepness contributes to the enhancement of the use of nutrients by plants as well as to the boost of plant returns by 43% in dry spell problems. Optimization of forms and sort of plant food placement in the dirt system and also feeding time in the vital stages of plant development, development of agrochemical history significantly enhance the stability of crop returns in different years by the hydrothermal conditions as well as boost their resistance to stress. Sustainable nutrient administration revolves around the non-excessive use of artificial or all-natural fertilizers.

This benefits both the farmer and the setting when correct methods are used. Improving the effectiveness of plant foods ought to decrease application rates and also prices while lowering the number of nutrients that can be shed to the environment through leaching, denitrification, or volatilization.

Of the four vital nutrients (nitrogen-N, phosphorous-P, potassium-K, and also sulfur-S) applied as synthetic plant food, N is the nutrient most easily lost. Nitrogen causes environmental damage and even economic loss to the farmer.

Nitrous oxide (N_2O) is one of the most potent farming greenhouse gas (GHG), having 298 times a lot more environmental influence per one molecule of gas than co2 (CO_2) In Manitoba, N_2O accounts for 66 percent of all farming GHG exhausts. Nitrogen is shed with several paths, increasing the chance of loss to the environment. A lot of injuries happen when way too much N fertilizer is used, and denitrification occurs. This nutrient can additionally be shed to groundwater or volatilized right into the atmosphere.

Any kind of plant food sources, such as decaying manure, synthetic fertilizer, or dirt N, can contribute to N losses. The positioning, timing, application technique, and price of compost or manure related to an area will influence the quantity of N readily available to the plant or lost to the atmosphere. Just concerning half of the N is made use of by the crop in the year of application. What takes place to the remaining N is uncertain. Depending upon ecological conditions and fertilizer placement and timing, the residual N could be immobilized (used up) by the dirt or shed to leaching, denitrification, and also volatilization. Typically, 2.7 percent of used plant food is discarded as N2O.

Complying with proper management techniques for both manure and plant foods can help reduced greenhouse gas discharges and represent financial savings for the farmer.

The last few years have tossed several cultivators a curveball in terms of weather condition patterns. From drought in 2012 throughout much of the Corn Belt to a too-wet-to-plant springtime in 2015 in several states, the only constant in the weather is that it's most likely to alter. Moisture and also temperature plays a significant role in the yield potential of crops, so understanding the interaction of climate and nutrients is a vital action in attaining higher returns as well as environmental stewardship.

Dampness is essential for the plant. It is needed for seed germination and also plants advancement. When planning plant food applications, check out the brief- and even lasting weather forecast for your area. Prompt and modest rains can be beneficial to liquefy dry plant food and also relocate nutrients right into the soil rooting area. However, extreme rainfall can raise runoff potential and seeping potential of nutrients such as nitrate, sulfate, chloride, and boron.

Plant water accessibility and nutrient schedule are also impacted by dirt structure. Coarser textured dirt does not have the water or nutrient capacity of silt loam soils. These soil types dry out faster and have a more severe danger for leaching, so necessary fertilizer needs to be split into 2-3 applications throughout the growing season.

In semi-arid and deserts, watering programs supply a

constant resource of much-needed water, which enables cultivators to manage dampness and also nutrient uptake. Nutrients such as potassium (K^+) regulate water within the plant, and even aid crops to endure dry spell and drier climates. On the other hand, areas that get high rains amounts basically period or have or have subsoils with high clay web content might need floor tile water drainage to move water off the surface and out of the rooting area to keep the great root and soil microbial health and wellness.

Temperature is likewise essential to plant physiology and also nutrient uptake. It affects chemical and even biological procedures within the dirt. Beginning with planting, temperature level drives seed germination, origin advancement, and nutrient uptake. Environments in southern areas of the UNITED STATE cozy before northern regions as well as allow for earlier planting dates as well as more extended growing periods. In contrast, north climates may experience cold springs that bring about slow seed germination, origin, and also plant advancement, and slow nutrient uptake contrasted to warmer years. Cozy temperature levels promote quick development of above- as well as listed below- ground plant advancement, leading to root expedition for nutrient uptake.

No matter location, functioning very carefully with an agronomist to attain balanced plant nourishment is the very best protection against the abrupt and also unanticipated modifications in the weather condition. Plants with appropriate food are healthy as well as can withstand anxieties incurred throughout the growing period.

CONCLUSIONS

House grow gardens and hydroponics can be a challenge when you are first beginning; once you have grown a couple of plants and also obtain used to the ins and outs of it, you will certainly see the distinction in your fruit and vegetables. Oh, did I mention that hydroponic crops create two times? Otherwise, three times faster than yard grew plants! It is sure to become your primary mode of horticulture from here on out. Just follow some basic tips and tricks for gardening and hydroponics, and you will see a visible distinction in your harvest.

Made in the USA
Middletown, DE
19 May 2020